LANDMARK VISITOR

Southe
Peak District

Lindsey Porter

Published By
Landmark Publishing Ltd
Waterloo House, 12 Compton, Ashbourne,
Derbyshire DE6 1DA England

Lindsey Porter has written many books on the Peak District – both guides & aspects of the area's history. His interests range from involvement in the Youth Hostels Association at a national level, photography and local history, especially of local customs & mining history. He is currently excavating a small disused copper mine & researching Shrovetide Football customs across the country.

He is married, with five children & two grandchildren.

His photography has been used on the cover of the YHA's Accommodation Guide, Annual Report and its Credit card

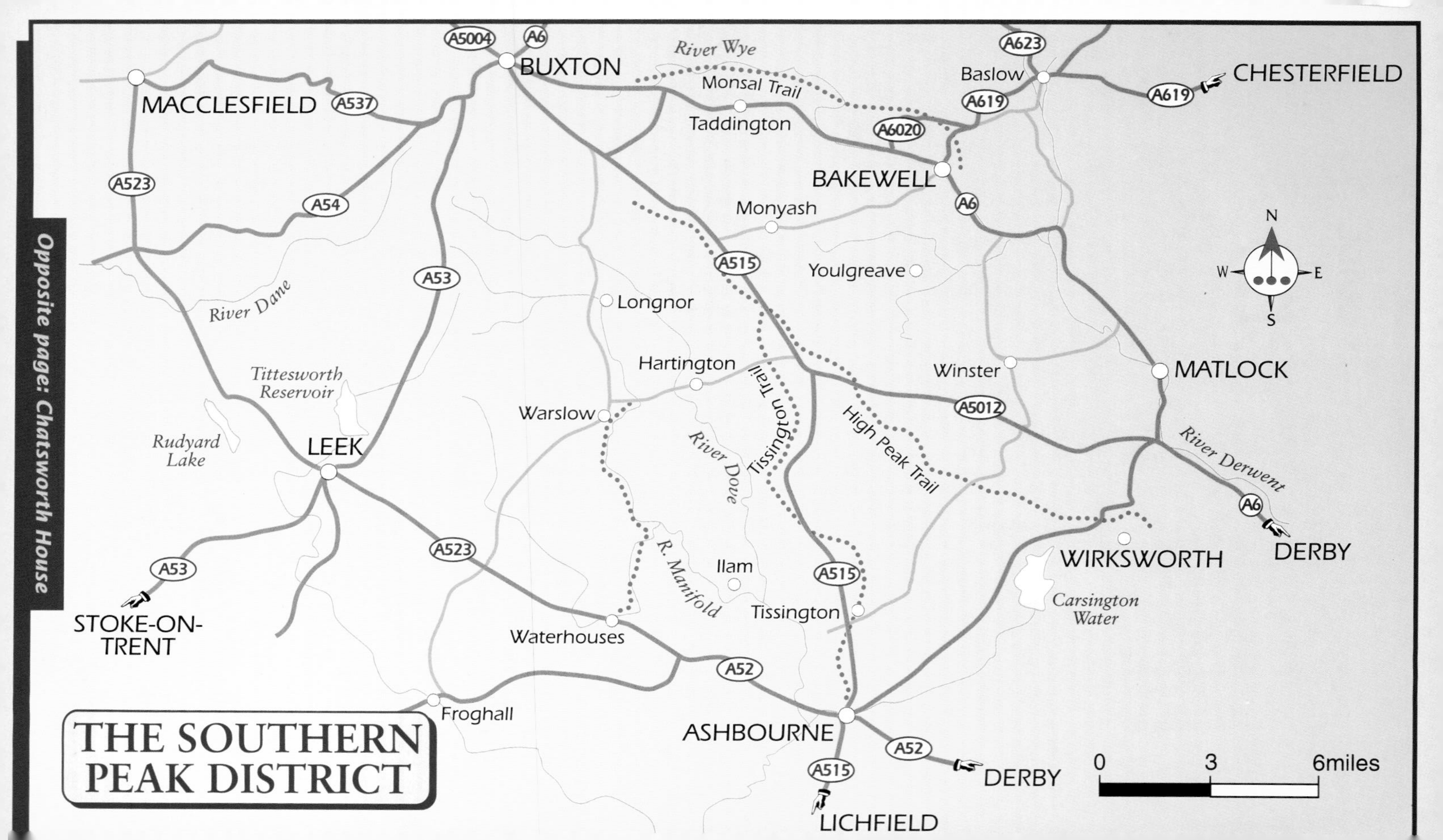

Opposite page: Chatsworth House

LANDMARK VISITORS GUIDE

Southern Peak District

Lindsey Porter

Contents

Introduction

The limestone uplands and dales of the Southern Peak District — the White Peak — are one of the most popular areas in the world. In fact, other than a national park in Japan, the Peak District receives more visitors than any other national park in the world.

There are so many visitors that on a sunny Bank Holiday, the number of cars create long tailbacks in the Matlock and Bakewell areas. The popular destinations of Hartington and Wetton Mill (in the Manifold Valley) suffer equally and can become gridlocked with cars.

Why then another book highlighting the attractions of this area? The answer lies in all those lovely areas which receive fewer visitors. By highlighting where these are and why they are worth visiting, this book shows how it is possible to have a day out in the Southern Peak without losing the quality of enjoyment we expect.

Further, by taking time to discover more of what the area has to offer, the level of enjoyment in and appreciation of the area is much enhanced.

Knowing how different are the habitats of Dovedale and Lathkill Dale (and why) for instance, lifts the enjoyment of walking along these dales. The Cromford/High Peak Wharf area is steeped in history as well as offering an area of diverse pleasant walks plus attractions ranging from the National Tramway Museum to the serene beauty of Lea Garden.

Each of the areas covered in this book offer you the opportunity of exploring in a much more satisfying way. Written by a local man with a deep knowledge of the Peak, you too can learn much more about the attractions and secrets of this lovely area. Whether you wish to explore on foot or by car, get to know the whole of the Southern Peak rather than its overcrowded honey-pots!

Left: When Edensor was rebuilt, the old pub was retained & refaced

• AUTHOR'S FAVOURITES •

Alton Towers

Britain's premier leisure park is situated south-west of Ashbourne. There are a substantial number of thrill-rides and a beautiful garden occupying both sides of a valley. Regrettably, there is no separate ticket for the garden. There is a hotel within the leisure park.

Carsington Water

Situated to the east of Ashbourne, this reservoir is now attracting about a million visitors per year. It is open all year round and there is a footpath for ramblers and cyclists of about 9 miles (14.4km) in length around the water. The Visitor Centre incorporates shops and a restaurant. Water sports equipment (including craft) and bikes may be hired.

Chatsworth*

The home of the Duke & Duchess of Devonshire, near Bakewell. Often termed "the Palace of the Peak", it is an apt description for this large, richly decorated house with a magnificent collection. The garden and park are also open to the public. The adjacent village of Edensor is also worth a visit.

National Tramway Museum, Crich*

A collection of over 50 restored trams, some from overseas, in a Victorian setting. Explore the street scene then take a ride on a tram for over a mile. You can also wander around the tram sheds and see restoration work in progress.

Cromford area

There is much to explore in and around Cromford especially concerning the heritage of industry and transport. Cromford was the home of Sir Richard Arkwright's cotton mills and the Arkwright Society is in the process of restoring his mill in Mill Lane.

You can visit the Cromford Canal and its wharf. At High Peak Junction is the canal-side terminus of the

Left: The Country Fair at Carsington Water
Right: Lea Gardens in late spring

Cromford & High Peak Railway with its buildings, including the oldest in situ railway line in the world. Dating from 1828, it carries the inscription 'C&HPR'.There are also two preserved stationary steam engines nearby. A bonus is the pleasant scenery in the area.

Lea Rhododendron Gardens

A remarkable oasis of beauty when the rhododendrons are in bloom. Over 500 species may be seen here.

Dovedale and the Manifold Valley

Two lovely limestone valleys which may be explored by footpaths. Dovedale has many tors and associated features rising from the ash woods which cover the valley sides. The old Manifold Valley Railway track is now tarmac surfaced and used by ramblers and cyclists (and cars between Swainsley and Redhurst Halt).

Haddon Hall*

This ancient house above the River Wye offers a complete contrast to the splendour of Chatsworth. Completed largely before the 17th century it is a remarkable survivor. The house is complimented by an award winning garden.

Heights of Abraham*

This interesting Visitor Centre has the most spectacular access — a cable car from nearby Matlock Bath railway station.

Lathkill Dale

This beautiful dale has completely different habitats on its two banks, due to being orientated east to west and the north side catching more sunshine.

Tissington Well Dressings

Blessed on Ascension Day, the ancient custom of dressing the wells attracts many visitors.

***Useful on a rainy day**

1 Western Valleys & Moors

The opening chapter explores the valleys of the rivers Dane and Churnet and surrounding moorland. The Dane has a lovely atmosphere while the Churnet although no longer the Secret Valley, as it used to be known, remains an area of relative peace and quiet. The moorland area north of Leek is very much quieter for those who seek the solitude of the open moors and upper reaches of the various rivers.

• ATTRACTIVE VALLEYS •

This area of the Peak District is an area of open and often treeless moorland dissected by two river systems — the Churnet and Dane. Flowing off the high moors, these two valleys offer good walking and extensive views. The huge outcrops of rocks known as the Roaches are perhaps the most notable geographical feature. Man has however added much else — interesting market towns, preserved mills, Tittesworth Reservoir, and the majestic Tudor Gothic mansion of Alton Towers.

There are no contrasting features like those found in the valleys of the Dove and Manifold, for instance, where sandstones and shales give way to the harder limestone. Here, all the rocks are varieties of sandstone and shales. It is therefore a different kind of topography moulded in softer rock than the limestone, creating rugged heather and bilberry-clad moors in the upper valleys. Further downstream, wooded and often deep, wide valleys are more characteristic.

The Staffordshire Moorlands

To the east rises the ridge known as Morridge, with the Mermaid Inn standing out on the treeless skyline. Just to the north of the inn is Blakemere, more popularly known as the Mermaid Pool, traditionally said to be bottomless and the home of a mermaid. It is strange that a pool very similar to this, known as Doxey Pool, also exists on the Roaches.

There is only limited parking on the narrow road which runs beneath the Roaches. However, there is now a free park-and-ride scheme which operates from **Tittesworth Reservoir** at weekends. Vehicles are left at the Meerbrook end, where there is a visitor centre close to the Meerbrook to Blackshaw Moor road.

Tittesworth Reservoir

Meerbrook, nr Leek. Visitor centre, fishing, sensory garden, children's play area, bird hide, coffee shop. Open all year, 7 days a week.
☎ 01538 300224.

If your route takes you up the Leek to Buxton road past Ramshaw Rocks, drive slowly looking for the rock which obviously resembles a face. Known as the Winking Eye rock, it does just that as you drive past it.

Below Tittesworth Reservoir, the river skirts the old market town of Leek. The river has for centuries been used for power and for its very pure qualities. The Cistercian monks built one of the largest abbey churches of their order in England on the banks of the River Churnet at Abbey Green, Leek and also established a watermill, presumably to grind corn. The abbey is no more, but a preserved cornmill still stands on the site of the original mill.

Below Cheddleton, where another preserved watermill exists, the valley is well wooded and remains so almost to Alton village where it becomes shallower. Although often neglected by visitors to the Peak District, this section is perhaps the prettiest part of the valley due to the lack of roads. Instead it is traversed by railway and canal, the latter adding to the tranquil atmosphere.

The valley of the River Dane is similar to the Churnet in that motor traffic is denied access to much of it. The river rises on Axe Edge above Three Shires Head and flows roughly westwards to the Cheshire plain where it meanders slowly towards the River Weaver. It has a tributary, the Clough Brook, which collects the waters from the Wildboarclough district; this is another large and beautiful valley or 'clough' worth exploring.

The road to Wincle at Danebridge

Compared with other areas of the Peak, there is not a great deal remaining of early occupation in this area. A notable exception is the prehistoric burial mound known as the Bridestones, situated at the southern end of the large hill, Bosley Cloud, close to the Congleton-Rushton-Leek road. It is a chambered burial tomb with some very tall standing stones. Visible from the road, it is accessible to the public and well worth examining.

Two churches of similar age to Leek are at Cheddleton and Horton, situated about 4 miles (6km) south and west of Leek respectively. Further north Rushton church, situated in the fields halfway between Rushton James and Rushton Spencer so as to serve both villages, is well worth a visit, as is the church in Forest Chapel north of Wildboarclough which was erected in 1673 and rebuilt in 1834. Here the annual rush laying ceremony can be observed.

• LEEK & THE CHURNET VALLEY •

The water of the valley spawned textile industries which developed to take advantage of its power and purity. Leek developed as a textile town producing silk. Dyestuffs were produced in great quantities, particularly in the nineteenth century when it was found that the water could be used to produce the raven-black dyes for which the town became so famous and which were so popular with the Victorians. Old textile mills mingle with silk workers' houses, but none are open to the public. Various 'mill shops' sell garments such as trousers, ladies' nightwear and underwear.

A walk around **Leek's** main streets reveals the Victorian influence particularly under the design of the Sugdens, a local firm of architects. In the Market Place is a **Butter Cross,** erected in 1671 and brought back to the Market Place in 1986 having been moved to the cemetery in 1857. The town's **cornmill** in Mill Street has been preserved and is worth a visit. It is claimed by enthusiasts to have been built by James Brindley, who had his workshops in the town. The waterwheel and all its machinery are intact and in working condition. Although

Brindley Water Mill

Mill Street, Leek.
Operational cornmill.
Museum of the life and times of James Brindley, engineer 1716-72 ☎ 01538 399332.
Open: Easter to end of September, weekends and Bank Holiday Mondays, 2pm–5pm; mid-July to end of August, also Monday, Tuesday and Wednesday 2pm–5pm.

better known as a canal engineer, his early career was as a millwright and he had close ties with the town.

An interesting phenomenon is sometimes observed from Leek churchyard between 20 and 22 June each year. At this time, if conditions are satisfactory, the sun will be seen to set completely behind Bosley Cloud then reappear from the side of Bosley Cloud's distinctive escarpment and finally set over the Cheshire plain. The double sunset can never be guaranteed because of cloud on the horizon, but many go to watch this spectacle each year.

Visitors are welcome at the **Coombes Valley Nature Reserve,** which protects woodland and pasture in the Coombes Valley, a tributary of the Churnet, between Cheddleton and Ipstones near to Leek.

The **Hawksmore Nature Reserve** near Oakamoor, on the road to Cheadle, also welcomes visitors. It is owned by the National Trust and a trail has been laid out in the extensive grounds which drop towards the Churnet.

Coombes Valley Nature Reserve

South of Leek, off A523 Leek to Ashbourne road. RSPB reserve with hides and woodland walks ☎ 01538 384017. Open: daily from 9am–9pm or dusk if earlier (closed 25 and 26 December). Small visitor centre open weekends and holiday periods.

Deep Hayes Country Park

Wallgrange, on the road to Cheddleton from Longsdon, south-west of Leek. Waymarked nature trail and information centre. Visitor Centre open: May-September, Saturday and Sunday, 2-5pm.

Ramshaw Rocks in August from the Leek – Buxton road

At **Cheddleton** on the A520 south of Leek is a preserved flint grinding mill. The picturesque site is adjacent to the Caldon Canal and a preserved narrow boat is moored here. Flint stones were calcined in kilns and ground to powder, then used in the Potteries to make bone china, hence its local importance. With two working waterwheels, the mill has become an important tourist attraction where the whole process is demonstrated.

Cheddleton Flint Mill & Boat Museum

Off Leek Road, Cheddleton. Working exhibitions of processing of materials for the pottery industry. Disabled access to ground floor only ☎ 01782 502907. Open: daily, Monday to Friday 10am–5pm, weekends 2pm–5pm.

Although one can no longer travel by British Rail in the immediate vicinity, two steam railway centres have been established. At Cheddleton, the old railway station about a mile downstream from the mill can be visited. It has a small collection of steam locomotives and rolling stock and a museum devoted to the North Staffordshire Railway.

A little further south at the **Foxfield Light Railway** near to Dilhorne, just off the Cheadle to Stoke-on-Trent road, you can also take a ride on a steam train for a few miles along a restored colliery line.

The Caldon Canal at Cheddleton

Churnet Valley Railway

Cheddleton Station, off A520 Leek to Stone road. Short train rides, some steam hauled, some diesel. Refreshment room and souvenir shop housed in ornate Victorian station building. Special events throughout the year. ☎ 01538 360522. Open: tearooms – weekends all year, plus every day in August. Shop – weekends all year plus Wednesdays in August. Telephone for details of train times.

Cheddleton to Froghall

The main appeal of the Churnet lies below Cheddleton, where the valley bottom can be followed along the canal towpath to Froghall. If you are particularly interested in canals and their architecture, take your car to **Denford**, just off the Leek to Hanley road (A53) at Longsdon. Walk westwards past the canal-side pub (The Hollybush) under the aqueduct which carries the Leek arm of the canal, to Hazelhurst locks. There is a canal keeper's cottage, a fine cast-iron footbridge and much to interest the photographer.

The Cheddleton to Froghall section really starts at Basford Bridge near the railway station. The valley is well wooded and the leafy glades provide a marvellous backcloth for the canal. **Consall Forge** is a small hamlet on the canal. Steep steps descend from each side of the valley to reach it, giving a more direct access than along the canal towpath. The hamlet gets its name from an old iron forge which existed in Elizabethan times, but all trace of it has long gone. Here, the canal and river run in one channel — a broad expanse of slow-moving water which separates again in front of the old canal pub, the Black Lion — now the preserve of ramblers and pleasure boat users.

The canal disappears under a footbridge and the railway, to meander casually down to Froghall and the wharf there. The river commences its own course once more at the foot of a large weir and the whole scene is worth stopping to examine and photograph. There is a Nature Centre situated on the road between Consall and Consall Forge.

Froghall to Alton

Two and a half miles further on is **Froghall** with its vast copper works and canal wharf. Here a picnic area has been created at the canal basin, and one can explore the old limekilns and loading docks where limestone was loaded onto railway wagons or into narrow boats. The quarry wagons ran on a 3ft 6in gauge track and lengths of rail of this gauge remain. With the 2ft 6in gauge of the Manifold Valley Light Railway and the standard gauge lines, the North Staffordshire Railway was the only railway company in Britain to have lines of three different gauges.

Although the valley between Froghall and **Oakamoor** is denied even to the rambler, the latter village is worth investigation. It has two old pubs and a picnic site on the foundations of an old copper works, demolished in 1963 and now consolidated at Froghall. Here Messrs Thomas Bolton & Sons manufactured the copper wire core for the first transatlantic cable in 1856. Other than a few date stones, nothing now remains of the works except for a very large mill pool, the retained water cascading down a stepped weir before disappearing under the road bridge.

The section of valley between Oakamoor and Alton offers a choice of routes. The road via Farley leaves the valley, affording views of the latter and the Weaver Hills. It goes through **Farley** village with its attractive cottages and beautiful hall, once the home of the Bill family. Beyond Farley, the views are towards **Alton Towers**, its turrets soaring above the trees.

Alton Towers

Alton, 3 miles (5km) east of Cheadle. ☎ 01538 702200. This huge mansion, formerly home of the Earls of Shrewsbury is today a gutted shell, but the grounds have been developed as a massive leisure park, on the Disneyland theme, with many attractions for young and old including its famous 'Nemesis' and 'Oblivion' rides. Billed as Europe's premier leisure park with over 120 rides, shows and other attractions, it includes the world's largest log flume 792m (2,600ft in length), a circus and two cineramas.Of particular interest are the gardens, once noted as the largest domestic gardens in Europe. Around the valley are many paths and steps and one can find a corkscrew fountain, a Gothic temple, a three-storey 'Stonehenge', a Swiss chalet, a huge range of conservatories and much use of water. In the summer one can often hear a band playing in the bandstand and, over the tree tops, see water shooting into the sky from a 'Chinese Pagoda' fountain, its gold painted bells glistening through the falling water. The gardens are particularly worth seeing in May when the rhododendrons are in flower.

Alton Towers is a big place attracting big crowds so go early in the morning. You may prefer to make your visit mid-week when there are sometimes fewer people about and less queuing for attractions. Single entrance fee covers all rides. Over 50 catering outlets, free parking, facilities for the disabled. Open: major rides and all attractions: mid-March to early November daily 10am-5, 6 or 7pm depending on season. Grounds and gardens: all year. Much reduced admission rate in winter payable at the on-site hotel (closed Christmas week).

The more direct route to Alton keeps to the valley bottom. On reaching the Former Pink Lodge, now a café and restaurant, one can walk westwards up **Dimmingsdale** to the former mill and its beautiful pools beyond. The café, now known as The Ramblers Retreat Coffee House, (☎ 01538 702730) is very popular in what used to be quite a quiet, secluded area. There is a large car park for visitors to Dimmingsdale adjacent to the café.

High Street, Alton, Staffs
☎ 01538 702065.
Open: every afternoon and Monday, Tuesday and Wednesday mornings.
Decorated earthenware, stoneware, sculpture.

Alton village once enjoyed the patronage of the Earls of Shrewsbury who owned almost everything in the area. Look out for the village lock-up and the castle.

The valley bottom at Alton has much to offer. The view up to the castle, perched high on the rocks above, looks like a Rhineland replica. The old railway station, built by Pugin, has been restored, while opposite is an old watermill.

• THE DANE VALLEY •

The Dane Valley, with its tributary the Clough Brook, rivals the Churnet and Dove Valleys as a major beauty spot in the west of the Peak District. Rising on Whetstone Edge, close to the Cat and Fiddle Inn, its deeply-cut valley confines the infant waters of the river. Using old packhorse routes as paths it is possible to walk down much of the valley. The old bridge at Three Shires Head should not be missed. Have a look underneath it to see that the bridge has been widened at some time either for increased horse traffic or for the passage of carts.

Highest village in England

A couple of miles downstream from the bridge is **Gradbach**, a scattered community with no village as such. It is easily approached off the A53 — the Leek to Buxton road — through **Flash**, which at 1,525ft (469m) is the highest village in England. This is a harsh village of weather worn cottages, huddled together on the side of Oliver Hill. Descending down to the Dane, the scenery is more interesting and the climate more tolerant.

Gradbach is worth taking time to explore. Lacking a village centre, it is best to park at the car park on the lane to the youth hostel and by the side of the river.

Look out for the old Methodist Chapel, built in 1849, and the adjacent cottage by the bridge over the river Dane, before walking downstream towards Gradbach Mill and Back Forest. The mill is easy to find, simply take the road to Flash from the bridge and turn first right down the side of a small brook. This is however a narrow road; once the car park is reached it is better to park there and walk.

Gradbach Mill, now owned by the Youth Hostels Association, used to be a silk mill with a large waterwheel fed by water from the Dane. It was rebuilt in 1758 following a fire, and closed down as a silk mill about 100 years later. Its large waterwheel was scrapped in the 1950s.

Lud Church

A good example of an old packhorse road can be seen ascending the hill on the opposite side of the river from the mill. Below the mill lie **Lud Church**, a gorge of considerable proportions high on the hillside, and Back Forest, a large wood which was stripped of its main timber in the mid-1950s. Lud Church repays the effort needed to reach it, preferably on a walk from Gradbach by way of Hanging Stone to Danebridge and Swythamley, a distance of approximately 8 miles (13km). In excess of 15m (50ft) deep and in places only a few feet wide, it became a meeting place of religious dissidents some 500 years ago and supposedly took its name from their leader.

Panniers Pool Bridge, Three Shires Head

Much of the area south of the river between Gradbach and Danebridge formed part of the Swythamley Estate which was divided and sold in 1977. The estate also included Swythamley Hall and the Roaches.

Wildboarclough

Further north under the hill of Shutlingsloe lies **Wildboarclough**. Taking the road westwards from Gradbach a couple of miles brings one to Allgreave where the minor road joins the A54. Just beyond the Clough Brook a minor road turns off to the right to run northwards towards

Shutlingsloe. This road hugs the brook all the way to Wildboarclough. It is an attractive route and passes the Crag Inn, a popular stopping-off place for visitors.

On the hillside above the post office is Crag Hall, the country seat of Lord Derby. Above the hall in the lane that leads northwards towards Bottom-of-the-Oven, look for the five horse troughs laid out in a semicircle. The roadway near the hall abounds with rhododendrons which are a riot of colour in early summer. If time permits, continue up-stream for half a mile or so and leave the car where the signpost indicates the path to Cumberland Clough. Walk up the brook past the deep ravine, with its rushing white water and dark conifers, to the waterfall before returning to the car.

Danebridge

Just above **Danebridge** the waters of the Clough and Dane unite to form a good sized river flowing beneath the broad arch after which the village takes its name. Like many neighbouring communities, Danebridge consists of a few loosely grouped cottages. It also has an interesting old pub, the Ship Inn, which until recently had some relics of Bonnie Prince Charlie's 1745 uprising, including a flintlock of a Scottish soldier and part of a newspaper he was carrying. The name Ship Inn is said to be a reminder of the *S S Swithamley* [*sic*], although the present inn sign is of the *Nimrod* which took Shackleton, and Sir Phillip Brocklehurst of Swythamley, to the Antarctic.

The broad fields below Danebridge, broken by areas of woodland and views of Bosley Cloud, make a pleasant walk to Gig Hall Bridge where the feeder channel to Rudyard reservoir starts. Above the valley is Wincle Grange Farm where the monks of old had a sheep and cattle farm.

From Gig Hall Bridge, the feeder supply winds down the valley to **Rushton**. It has a path at the side, much in the nature of a towpath, which provides a pleasant walk. Below the village lies Rudyard Lake, built by John Rennie as a water supply to the Trent and Mersey Canal and today a popular resort for yachtsmen and fishermen.

Shutlingsloe from the path to Gradbach from the Crag Inn

WALKS IN THE CHURNET & DANE VALLEYS

Churnet Valley

There are a variety of walks which enable the valley to be seen at its best, particularly as the beauty spots are, for the most part, denied to the motorist. The canal towpath from Froghall, can be used to gain access to Consall Forge. Alternatively there are two paths which descend more directly to the hamlet. The towpath from Froghall, as distinct from the path from Cheddleton which can be muddy, is useful for pushing wheelchairs, although there is a bridge with steps to cross.

The more direct paths descend to the Churnet from Consall village and from Belmont. In each case there are numerous steps to descend but Consall Forge is well worth the effort. Park in Consall village and walk eastwards towards the valley. At a bend in the road, a signpost to Consall Forge indicates the start of a well-used path which crosses fields before descending down into the valley for 1.5 miles (2km).

The more interesting route to the river is from Belmont pools, down the 'Devil's Staircase'. The 200 steps descend from the wood near Belmont pools through the estate of Belmont Hall (not open to the public). Park at Belmont pools on the Cheddleton to Ipstones road. The path (not the hall drive) is taken to Consall Forge. The pools are popular with photographers — the huge beech trees create a perfect setting for the artificial pools.

Dane Valley

A recommended 9 mile (14.5km) circular route takes in the Dane and Clough Brook. For convenience, start at Wildboarclough where there is adequate roadside car parking. Just upstream of the Crag Inn take the footbridge over the brook and climb over the hill to the main road (A54) and Tagsclough Hill. From here, this old packhorse route continues straight to Gradbach Mill via Burntcliff Top. It emerges at the Flash to Allgreave road by the side of an old pub, the Eagle and Child, now a private house. Inside the entrance is a plaque depicting an eagle and child taken from the arms of the Stanleys, Earls of Derby, who own Crag Hall and its estate at Wildboarclough.

From Gradbach Mill proceed upstream to the chapel where a path cuts up the hill east of the Dane to Turn Hill where it meets the packhorse route to Three Shires Head from Flash. Cross the bridge at Three Shires Head and continue over to Cumberland Clough via Holt Farm and the western edge of Dane Bower. Follow the clough down to the road and turn downstream to Wildboarclough.

2 The Goyt Valley & Macclesfield

The Goyt starts close to the Dane in the wide expanse of peat bogs north of Three Shires Head. Once the tree line is reached the valley becomes of more interest, but its physical character is lost beneath the waters of Fernilee and Errwood reservoirs. To the west rises Shining Tor and the exposed edge of gritstone known as Windgather Rocks. Despite much of it being flooded, there is plenty of interest in the Goyt Valley and the surrounding area.

To the west lies **Macclesfield Forest** and the high moorland of Shining Tor. The road upstream from Wildboarclough can be used as a good introduction to the area. Turn first left (above the village, opposite Dryknowle Farm). The road soon enters the forest to pass between **Trentabank and Ridgegate Reservoirs.**

Trentabank Visitor Centre

Small snack bar, car park, toilets, several woodland trails and a large heronry.

At the road junction opposite the pub turn right up the narrow road which climbs steeply uphill. The narrow road climbs up to the hamlet of Macclesfield Forest with its rugged chapel and school. The **Forest Chapel**, a low and simple building with an equally small bell tower, is well known for its Rush Bearing Service. On the nearest Sunday to 12 August, the chapel floor is strewn with rushes and a service is held in the afternoon, attended by many people.

Continue to Bottom-of-the-Oven and then drive up the lane northwards to **Lamaload Reservoir.** It has a picnic area at its northern end which is a quieter stopping place than at Errwood Reservoir, in the Goyt Valley.

Jenkin Chapel

From Lamaload proceed to **Jenkin Chapel** which, according to the tablet, was built at John Slack's expense in 1733. The short tower was added in 1755. The chapel looks more like a house than a religious building, and even the interior has a homely feel about it with its compactness and box pews. It was built alongside an important saltway. Just to the

Below: The Upper Goyt Valley below Derbyshire Bridge

south is Saltersford Hall, a reminder of the days when packhorses with panniers loaded with salt made their way towards the Peak. An open air service is held here on the second Sunday in September at 3pm.

Goyt Valley

Turn eastwards and climb over **Pym Chair** before dropping down to the twin reservoirs of Errwood and Fernilee. Looking across the dam between the reservoirs the steep inclined road, leading up to the Buxton to Whaley Bridge road, was formerly part of the Cromford and High Peak Railway and wagons used to be hauled up the incline by a steam engine at the top. The reservoir at the top of the incline provided water for the engine's boiler.

The ruins of Errwood Hall near the south-western end of the water are an interesting detour, particularly when the rhododendrons are in bloom. A gunpowder works used to operate nearby many years ago. There are two picnic areas by Errwood Reservoir, one in the wood at the Errwood end of the road from Jenkin Chapel and the other at the upper end of the reservoir close to the ruins of Errwood Hall. A forest trail links up with this picnic area. Yachting takes place on Errwood Reservoir.

The road from here gradually climbs up Goyt's Clough past Goytsclough Quarry, where there are more picnic tables. It reaches **Derbyshire Bridge**, moved upstream when the reservoirs were built, to meet an old road known as Jagger's Gate. To the west on the open moorland is the **Cat and Fiddle Inn**, built in 1831. Second to Tan Hill, it is the highest pub in England, standing at 515m (1,690ft) above sea level.

Just above Derbyshire Bridge the Macclesfield to Buxton road (A537) has a junction with the road to Congleton (A54). If you head towards Congleton, you pass an old chimney on your left before reaching a right turn which leads down into the beautiful Wildboarclough.

Macclesfield

Macclesfield is an old textile town which expanded following the building of the Macclesfield Canal and later the railway. Of particular interest to visitors is the **Silk Mill and Heritage Centre** — the first museum in Britain to be devoted to the silk industry. Housed in the former Sunday School, it includes a restored Victorian classroom.

Nearby **Paradise Mill** may dispute the Silk Mill and Heritage Centre's claim to fame, for it is a working museum of the town's former silk industry. Twenty six hand-powered Jacquard looms survive and are used to demonstrate the skills of a dying craft.

Just to the north of the town centre is West Park, one of the earliest public parks, dating from 1854. Situated within it is the **West Park Museum** housing a wide range of fine and decorative art material and objects relating to local history.

Paradise Silk Mill

Park Lane ☎ 01625 618228. Exhibitions and room settings. Museum shop. Admission fees charged. Open: Tuesday to Sunday 1–5pm. Closed Mondays (except Bank Holidays), New Year's Day, Good Friday, Christmas Day and Boxing Day.

West Park Museum

Prestbury Road, Macclesfield ☎ 01625 619831.
Small but significant collection of Egyptian antiquities.
Venue for a variety of touring exhibitions.
Open: Tuesday to Sunday 2–5pm, closed Mondays (except Bank Holidays), 1 Jan, Good Friday, Christmas Day and Boxing Day.

Left: Descending into the Goyt Valley from Pym Chair

Right: Gradbach

Between Macclesfield and Macclesfield Forest is the **Tegg's Nose Country Park**, based around an old sandstone quarry. A static exhibit about the quarry uses some of the original equipment, and there are various walks which start from the car park. Another walk is the **Middlewood Way**, a reclaimed railway line 11 miles (17.7km) long between Macclesfield and Middlewood, which is useful for cycling and horse riding, or it can be used as part of a circular path incorporating the Macclesfield Canal or the Gritstone Trail.

Bollington Discovery Centre

Grimshaw Lane, Bollington ☎ 01625 572681. Visitor centre alongside Macclesfield Canal and Middlewood Way. Cycle and canoe hire. Open: Easter to end of October, weekends and Bank Holidays, Saturday 12–6pm, Sunday 10.30am–6pm. Weekdays during July and August, 10.30am–6.pm.

The **Gritstone Trail** is a 20 mile (32km) path from Lyme Park near Disley, to Rushton near Leek. It links with the Staffordshire Way to make a long distance path and passes through Tegg's Nose Country Park. A leaflet about the trail is available from nearby tourist information centres. Both these trails have memorable views in almost all directions.

The Macclesfield area has several country houses open to the public. **Adlington Hall** to the north dates mainly from the fifteenth century, with a Regency south front. It is a beautiful half-timbered house set in fine grounds. The great hall is a particularly interesting survival, while the Georgian barn is now a tearoom.

Capesthorne Hall

Siddington. Georgian chapel, Mill Wood Walk, gardens with nature trail (suitable for wheelchairs), park and lakes, café and craft shop. 30 pitches for touring caravans/tents ☎ 01625 861221. Caravans and camping ☎ 01625 861779. Open: March to October inclusive, Sundays and Wednesdays and all Bank Holidays (except Christmas and New Year). Park, gardens and chapel 12noon–6pm; hall 1.30–4.30pm. Last admission to hall at 3.30pm.

Gawsworth Hall

Gawsworth, 22 miles (35km) south of Macclesfield on the A536. Striking fifteenth century half-timbered hall with beautiful gardens. Open-air theatre with covered grandstand, mid-June to mid-August. ☎ 01260 223456. Open: Easter to early October, daily 2–5.30pm.

Lyme Hall featured in the recent TV adaptation of Jane Austen's *Pride and Prejudice*. The drive and south front were used for shooting scenes of *Pemberley*, Mr Darcy's house. The garden, pool and south front were clearly recognisable.

Lyme Hall and Park

Disley, on A6, 62 miles (10km) from Stockport. Park open all year round, 1,300 acre (520 hectare) with red and fallow deer. 17 acres of historic gardens. Hall with guides in Edwardian servant's costumes Tearoom and shop. ☎ 01663 762023. Open: Easter to end of October, 1.30–5pm Saturday to Wednesday. Bank Holidays 11am–5pm.

Left: Forest Chapel, Macclesfield Forest

3 Dovedale & Manifold Valley

Opposite: The path through Dovedale, just south of Mill Dale

Both the Rivers Dove and Manifold rise on the grits and shales of Axe Edge, in close proximity to each other and to the Rivers Goyt, Dane and Wye which divide this bleak upland area into different watersheds. All these rivers flow down deeply incised courses contrasting with the shallow valley of the River Hamps, the main tributary of the Manifold.

Limestone reef knolls

The upper reaches of both the Dove and the Manifold are spectacular. Take the Hollinsclough road from the Traveller's Rest Inn. The road soon climbs Edge Top where one can pull off the road and view both valleys at the same time. At this point the Manifold has cut deeply into the gritstone formations but the more spectacular view is towards Hollinsclough and the hills beyond. It is here that the overlying grits are replaced by the older limestones. These are chiefly bedded, but characteristic of this side of the limestone and gritstone boundary are the limestone reef knolls which have not yet yielded in the same way to the forces of erosion.

The result is a succession of hills on the edge of the limestone plateau which stretch down the Dove and the Manifold. Examples include Hollins Hill, Chrome Hill, Parkhouse Hill, High Wheeldon, Thorpe Cloud, and Thor's Cliff. These are the closest approximations to 'peaks' in the Peak District. The fossil content of these rocks also differs.

Beyond Hollinsclough, the character of the two valleys changes. The Dove flows through a deep limestone valley past Crowdecote towards Hartington, while the Manifold, still flowing across the softer overlying shales, occupies a very broad and shallow valley. This difference can easily be seen by taking the Longnor to Sheen road, running along the rounded bluff between the rivers that at one point are less than a mile apart.

Limestone dales

Below Hartington and Hulme End, both rivers occupy gorge-like valleys cut deeply into the limestone. The broad valley of the Manifold suddenly ends at the huge limestone dome of Ecton Hill. Hereafter it is characterised by huge incised meanders (a geological term approximating to large loops in a river found in a

deep gulley rather than a flat meadowland) until the two rivers unite. It is these meanders ('many folds') which give the river its name, and they create an ever-changing subject for the eye and camera. As a result the scenery is more varied than the Dove Valley until one reaches the Milldale to Thorpe Cloud section of the River Dove.

This is Dovedale — a majestic stretch of the valley now unfortunately suffering from overuse by ramblers. With its natural ashwoods, numerous towers of natural stone and features such as Pickering Tor, The Twelve Apostles, Reynard's Arch and Ilam Rock, it has much to commend it. Dovedale is protected by the National Trust and the dale forms the major part of the Trust's South Peak Estate.

Disappearing rivers

One of the main tributaries of these two rivers is the Hamps which flows off Morridge near to Leek, in a very broad valley to Waterhouses where it too reaches the limestone and enters a deeply incised valley like the Manifold. An unusual feature of both the Hamps and the Manifold is the disappearance of the water during dry spells. The Hamps is swallowed up at Waterhouses down solution cavities in the limestone known as 'swallets' or elsewhere in the Peak as 'shackholes'. There are more swallets at Wetton Mill and at Redhurst, just before the Wetton road begins to climb out of the valley. Both rivers occupy different underground channels and do not appear to unite. Coloured dyes take some 22-24 hours to re-emerge at the boil-holes in the grounds of Ilam Hall, close to the riverside path.

Compleat Angler

Perhaps the greatest name associated with the Dove is that of Izaak Walton who used to stay with his close friend — who became his adopted son — Charles Cotton. Cotton added chapters to Walton's *Compleat Angler* in the fifth edition before Walton died, his fame assured. Beresford Hall estate, through which flowed the Dove, was owned by Cotton. Beresford Dale is one of the prettiest places on the whole of the river, although Dutch Elm disease has killed many trees and their removal has marred the dale.

Much of the stone for dry stone walls was quarried locally and many small quarries and limekilns can be found. There are several, for instance, in Hartington Dale between the village and its old railway station. It was quite common for a farmer to have his own limekiln to burn stone for his land.

Cheese making

Close to Beresford Dale is Hartington, where the cheese factory, the last in Derbyshire, now owned by Mendip Dairy Crest, makes blue and white Stilton cheese which is exported all around the world. It also manufactures Buxton Blue which has an orange colour to it, Dovedale Blue which is softer and more creamy than ordinary Stilton, and Blue Wensleydale.

Hartington Cheese Shop

By the village pond (mere), Market Place, Hartington
☎ 01298 84935. Cheese fresh from the factory next door. Open: all year, Monday to Friday 9am – 12.30pm and 1–5pm: Saturday and Sunday 9am – 12.30pm and 1–4pm.

Abandoned railways

Despite being so rural, the area was served by three railway lines. The Buxton to Ashbourne line was the most recent, for work commenced as late as 1890. At Parsley Hay it joined the Cromford and High Peak Railway for a while before leaving the latter to enter Buxton. The Cromford and High Peak Railway was built much earlier.

Of more interest perhaps is the narrow gauge (30in) railway that ran down the Hamps Valley and up the Manifold Valley from Waterhouses to Hulme End. This railway opened in 1904 and ran for 30 years. It was an unusual railway, with locomotives modelled on those from a narrow gauge line in India. All three lines are now trails for walks and cyclists.

***Right:* Wolfscote Dale**

***Opposite page:* Viator Bridge, Mill Dale**

RAILWAY TRAILS

The **Manifold Valley Trail** commences at Waterhouses, initially following the Hamps Valley. It is very picturesque and equally enjoyable, whether on foot or on a bike. The latter is a useful means of travelling up the valley to Hulme End, a distance of eight miles. The first station was at Sparrowlea, where there is a tearoom in the adjacent farmhouse.

After four miles is Beeston Tor, the large cliff of reef limestone opposite the farm, where the Hamps Manifold Valleys join. It was here that Saxon coins and jewellery were found during an archaeological dig in 1924. The finds are now in the British Museum.

The trail continues past Weag's Bridge and Thor's Cave to Redhurst, where the old line is shared with vehicles to Swainsley. There is a tearoom at Wetton Mill near to the swallet holes where the river dives underground. Some of these may be seen from the road at Redhurst.

Swainsley Tunnel is now lit for safety and here the railway line runs on to Hulme End without vehicular traffic (except for access to land). You can park at Hulme End, Swainsley, Wetton Mill, Weag's Bridge and Waterhouses.

The old booking office and engine shed remain at Hulme End and the former has recently been restored. The Manifold Valley Hotel in the hamlet used to be known as the Light Railway Hotel. It serves food and makes a useful place to relax before returning down the valley.

The **Tissington Trail** runs north of Ashbourne. It is a climb uphill north of here onto the limestone plateau, but thereafter, it is much easier! There are car parks at Tissington, Alsop-en-le-Dale, Hartington and Parsley Hay. Hartington Station lies 1.5 miles (2.4km) from the village. The trail has good views across the southern Peak District and ends north of Hurdlow Station. Here the line is still in use by the neighbouring limestone quarries. The line north of Parsley Hay was part of the Cromford and High Peak Railway and the trail continues as the High Peak Trail north of

Left: Hartington Signal Box, Tissington Trail
Right: Manifold Valley Trail, Hulme End Station & Visitors' Centre

Parsley Hay. This latter trail ran down to the Derwent Valley and High Peak Junction.

South of Parsley Hay, parts of both trails are now nature reserves. On the High Peak Trail, either side of the A515 are large beds of heather. Limestone heathland is now quite rare and most of the areas in which it occurs are protected. Look at the plaques on the bridge carrying the A515. One is dated 1825, which makes this one of the oldest lines in the country.

The **High Peak Trail** is very flat, other than the inclines. It passes Friden Brickworks before reaching the A5012 near Pikehall. At Gotham, the line nearly turns through a right angle in a 55yd (51m) radius, an amazing feature which meant large locomotives could not be used on the line. There are parking and picnic tables at Friden Station as well as Minninglow, near to Gotham Curve.

Beyond Minninglow, look out for several large stonefaced embankments built to keep the line flat. Below Minninglow itself (the site of a chambered tomb) is an old quarry served by the line. The trail winds its way through Longcliffe and more quarries to the Hopton incline. Originally worked by a stationary haulage engine, this incline was sufficiently shallow for later locomotives to climb it unassisted (the gradient was 1:14). It was the steepest unassisted incline on British Railways. Having levelled out once more, the line runs on to Middleton Top Engine house from where the line descends steeply down Middleton and Sheep Pasture inclines to the Derwent Valley at High Peak Junction.

The Monsal Trail runs between Blackwell Mill Junction (near Topley Pike and 3 miles (4.8km) east of Buxton) and Coombes viaduct, one mile south-east of Bakewell. Four tunnels have been closed on the grounds of safety and it is necessary to follow a diversion which is clearly marked. The old railway line was cut high on the valley side above the River Wye and is now a pleasant walk with memorable views. There are car parks at the former stations at Bakewell and Millers Dale and also near Topley Pike.

The Bakewell to Longstone section is suitable for cyclists and horse riders. For the disabled, there are level surfaces in either direction from Bakewell and Millers Dale stations.

• THE RIVER DOVE •

Although initially only a small stream, the River Dove has a pronounced valley within half a mile or so of its source. It flows below Brand Top, where the simple war memorial records the loss of five men from one family. There are a lot of packhorse routes in this area and footpaths now follow these old trails.

Several cross the infant river with a single large slab of stone acting as bridges. A substantial, virtually disused packhorse bridge survives at Washgate, 2 miles (3.2km) below the source. It has low walls to allow uninterrupted passage of the horses and their side panniers.

The Upper reaches

The Dove Valley is unusual in that it is possible to walk down the first 20 miles (32km) of its course, all the way to Ashbourne. You need to use the 1:25000 Ordnance Survey White Peak Map and do it in stages, perhaps as circular walks or with a car waiting ahead.

Below Glutton, the small river trickles along in a deep and fairly wide valley. The harder limestone rocks on the east side are higher than the softer gritstones on the west side. It is relatively quiet all the way down the valley to Hartington where the tourists flock daily. The walking is very pleasant too, through pasture and on farm tracks or quiet lanes. There is a pub — The Packhorse — at Crowdecote, where you can relax before continuing on towards Pilsbury and Hartington.

At **Pilsbury**, there is a motte and bailey castle with an interpretation board, explaining a little about this Norman fortification. Look out for Broadmeadow Hall on the west or Staffordshire side of the valley. It is seventeenth century and was on the Peak Park's endangered buildings list until its use changed from a barn back to a rather fine looking dwelling.

Hartington

Hartington is situated where Hartington Dale joins the Dove. The River Hardin which runs down Hartington Dale has a subterranean course and is culverted under Hartington's Market Place. There is a pottery producing terracotta ware and

Rookes Pottery

Mill Lane, Hartington

☎ 01298 84650. Terracotta garden pottery made on the premises. Visitors may look round the workshop and see pots in production. Open: weekdays 9am–5pm, Saturday 10am–5pm, Sunday 11am–5pm. Closed weekends in January and February.

the Sheepskin and Tapestry Shop sells quality ladies wear. Hartington also benefits from the Dales Gift Shop, various tearooms, two pubs and a bookshop in the old chapel.

The church has some remnants of early decorated plasterwork and the Hall, built in 1611, is claimed to be the best surviving example of a Derbyshire yeoman's house. It was the home of the Bateman family. The other wings were added in 1861 while the farm buildings were built in 1859. The west bays were added in 1911 on the house's 300th anniversary. It is now a youth hostel offering private rooms, some en-suite, as well as more traditional dormitory accommodation.

Tissington Trail

The former Hartington railway station is now a picnic site with toilet facilities, while the railway track has been converted into the **Tissington Trail**. There is an information centre in the old signal box which still retains its original lever frames, and several photographs on the wall show what the railway used to look like. The trail gives level walking and cycling north from Ashbourne. Cycles may be hired from the National Park at Parsley Hay Wharf (SK147636) and Ashbourne (SK175470). If you hire a cycle from Parsley Hay and end up in Hartington, it is better to return via Long Dale, as it is a much easier gradient. Proceed eastwards out of the village, past the school and take the first turn to the left, into Long Dale. Sections of this valley are part of the Derbyshire Dales National Nature Reserve.

The Dales

Below Hartington, the valley becomes a gorge, the meadows ending abruptly at **Beresford Dale.** Charles Cotton lived in Beresford Hall, but it had become a ruin by 1850 and has now gone completely. Look out for the Prospect Tower rebuilt in 1905-6 with stone from the remains of the hall, and also for the fishing temple. The latter, dating from 1674, is on private land but can be seen from the footpath as one approaches the trees at the north end of the dale from Hartington. Cotton also owned Throwley Hall (the ruins of which can be seen from the Calton to Ilam road) but both Beresford and Throwley Halls are now no more.

The valley is deeper in the next dale, **Wolfscote Dale**, and the character stays like this all the way to beyond **Mill Dale**, where it becomes more wooded. Mill Dale is a popular place, despite being very small. It has a small shop that also sells refreshments, car park and toilets.

The valley path uses the road between Lode Mill (a lead smelter built in 1760) and Mill Dale. However a path runs along the top of the valley from Mill Dale to the Lode Mill to Alsop-en-le-Dale road with splendid views down into the dale. The National Trust rightly has resisted pressure to open the other side of the river to ramblers — it is the last piece of limestone pasture in the valley on the Derbyshire side to remain without a path. Here is a good case of conservation taking priority over visitors.

Dovedale

Below Mill Dale lies **Dovedale**, with its limestone tors and relict ashwood, now a Grade 1 Site of Special Scientific Interest. The valley is very popular, and a causeway built along the pathway seems to contain the pressure from over a million visitors each year. The area around the tall Ilam Rock is particularly scenic. There is a footbridge here and land on which to sit and absorb the beauty around you. The bridge takes one over to the path in Hall Dale and affords an opportunity to watch the fish and wild ducks on the river. The freestanding tors in Dovedale are probably the tallest in the Peak District.

Below Ilam Rock are Pickering Tors, the Lion Head Rock, Tissington Spires and Lovers Leap before one reaches the **Stepping Stones** and the end of the gorge. The valley then becomes much more shallow as it continues on to Coldwall Bridge — a huge and unused turnpike era road bridge — Mappleton and the Okeover estate.

Crystal clear water

The section between Beresford Dale and the Stepping Stones differs from the rest of the valley. The river is flowing across a gravelly limestone river bed, the water is crystal clear and the path tends to hug the river. It therefore creates more interest than walking through the middle of river meadows, which characterises the rest of the Dove and the Manifold/Hamps light railway trail.

At the Stepping Stones you can leave the Dove and climb up Lin Dale to reach Thorpe and the Peveril of the Peak Hotel which is built at the side of the footpath. When most visitors came by train (or on foot) from Ashbourne, this was the main way to Dovedale. Beyond the Stepping Stones, the river joins the Manifold below the Izaak Walton Hotel. The dining room here looks out onto Dovedale and has one of the best views from any hotel dining room in the country.

• THE RIVER HAMPS •

West of Dove Dale lies the Manifold Valley and the upper basin of the River Hamps. Paths across the area are recommended to ramblers and it is easy to organise a circular route. There are many paths in this valley all the way down to Winkhill on the A523, where the valley becomes flat and featureless before turning north and into the limestone. At Mixon there are the remains of an old copper mine which was last worked in 1858. North of the mine are two nineteenth century dams, although they no longer impound water. They remain as relics of the old mine.

Cycle Hire at Waterhouses

1. Peak Cycle Hire, Old Station Car Park ☎ 01538 308609. Open daily, April to September, weekends and holidays October to March (check availability), 9.30am–6pm (dusk if earlier).

2. Brown End Farm, Leek Road ☎ 01538 308313. Open: Easter to October. 9.30am–7pm, otherwise by arrangement.

Spring is a good time of year for walking here. Marsh marigolds and lady smocks add a splash of colour to the lush vegetation as one strolls along in quiet and unspoilt surroundings. Downstream there is little of interest in Onecote village, but the small collection of houses in Ford 1.5 miles (2.4km) further downstream is often missed by visitors and is a very tranquil spot.

The River Hamps changes its character completely at **Waterhouses**, where it leaves the grit and shales and enters limestone country. The river often disappears underground for months on end in dry weather, but rises again at Ilam. The track bed of the old light railway runs up the valley from Waterhouses and may be used by walkers or cyclists. The best way to return is down the same track; there is as much of interest travelling back as one sees when travelling up the valley, although the exposed limestone cliffs and caves are a feature not of the Hamps but of the Manifold Valley.

The cycle track up the former Manifold railway line passes Sparrow Lee Farm, where refreshments are available

• THE RIVER MANIFOLD •

The River Manifold flows off the gritstone moors and runs close to the River Dove as far as Longnor. The main packhorse route between Flash and Longnor is now tarmac covered and runs along the aptly named Edge Top, giving marvellous views down into the deep valley that carries the infant waters of the Manifold towards Longnor. Beyond the valley is the moor of Middle Hills and Flash village, the highest village in England.

Longnor is a compact village built of local stone mined at Daisy Knoll, on the Hollinsclough road. Even the bricks of the Crewe and Harpur Arms were made locally, at Reapsmoor, 3 miles (2.4km) to the south. Longnor is not at all pretentious, but it is none the worse for that. The Market Hall, dated 1873 and now housing a very pleasant craft centre, still retains its toll board for buyers and sellers at nineteenth century Longnor markets and fairs. A recent development has been the small industrial estate near the fire station where clock manufacture is an unusual industry, but one not unknown to the region. The village, with its four pubs serving food, is a useful centre for exploring the upper reaches of the Manifold and Dove valleys.

Longnor Craft Centre

Market Hall. Exhibits and sale of work, including traditional furniture, by local craftspeople and artists. Cakes and snacks are available, including 'oaties'. Made in nearby Warslow, these have a variety of fillings in a traditional north Staffordshire oatcake. They are well worth a try! ☎ 01298 83587. Open: March-December daily 10am-5pm; January and February, Saturday and Sunday only.

Below Longnor the valley widens out into flat riverside meadows that are used for haymaking. Although it is not possible to walk down the valley to Longnor, below the village, paths and minor roads can be taken to walk to Hulme End. Ahead lies the rounded form of

Above: Wetton Opposite page: Alstonfield

Ecton Hill, heralding the start of the limestone and the more attractive section of the valley.

At **Ecton** are the remains of the old copper mine. Today, the mines are quiet and the shafts flooded. Above river level, a generation of mining-industry students have used the hillside and its workings for practical fieldwork. Discerning ramblers use the paths over the hill, the extensive views stretching far away in all directions.

Today, many visitors wend their way to **Wetton Mill** and on to **Thor's Cave**, past limestone crags and the water swallets that take all the river water except in winter and periods of heavy rain. Thor's Cave rises 350 ft (107m) high above the river, its 60ft (18m) entrance a disappointing promise of a good cave system beyond.

Beyond Thor's Cave is Weag's Bridge and Beeston Tor, where the Manifold meets the Hamps. From here there is no path down the valley floor. A lane climbs from Ilam to Throwley, where the old hall remains have been stabilised and a path from Wetton to Castern cuts across the valley rim above the nature reserve. Both give glimpses into what must be the prettiest dale in the Peak without access to the public — and long may it remain so.

Beyond is Ilam and the merging of the Dove and Manifold, the latter losing its name to the Dove which has been, and continues to be, the county boundary, despite being the minor of the two rivers.

4 Ashbourne & around

'The Gateway to Dovedale' is how Ashbourne describes itself although the Dove skirts the town centre as it flows from Ilam down to Hanging Bridge on the outskirts of the town. Primarily a market town, it retains many eighteenth century buildings together with other much older buildings in its main streets such as the Gingerbread Shop which is timber framed and thought to be fifteenth century. The Italian Restaurant in the Butchery is of a similar age. It is probable that the town was originally situated further to the west and nearer the church which is now almost out of the town, but development of a new centre, including the market place, probably began as early as the thirteenth century.

In the main street

Places to look out for in the town include the **Green Man and Black's Head Royal Hotel**. Its inn sign stretches over the street, and it has a small courtyard where coaches unloaded. Look at the Black's Head carved on the gallows-style inn sign; on one side he smiles, on the other he is sad. Of Georgian origin, the inn has associations with Boswell, who along with Dr Johnson stayed in the town with Dr Taylor who owned The Mansion in Church Street. **The Mansion House** is of seventeenth century origin with a brick facade, and a porch similar to the Grey House opposite, dating from the mid-eighteenth century. Next door to the Mansion is the Old House, also built in the eighteenth century. Offering bed and breakfast, it has a good reputation and is recommended.

A walk along the street towards the church is very rewarding. There are many Georgian houses of interest including No 61, The Grey House, which is next to the **Old Grammar School**. Sir Nikolaus Pevsner described Church Street as one of the finest streets in Derbyshire. The Grammar School was founded in 1585. The central portion with four gables above was the old schoolroom and the schoolmaster's accommodation was at either side, while opposite are the almshouses built in 1614-30.

Below: St Oswald's Parish Church. Its spire reaches a height of 64m (212 ft)

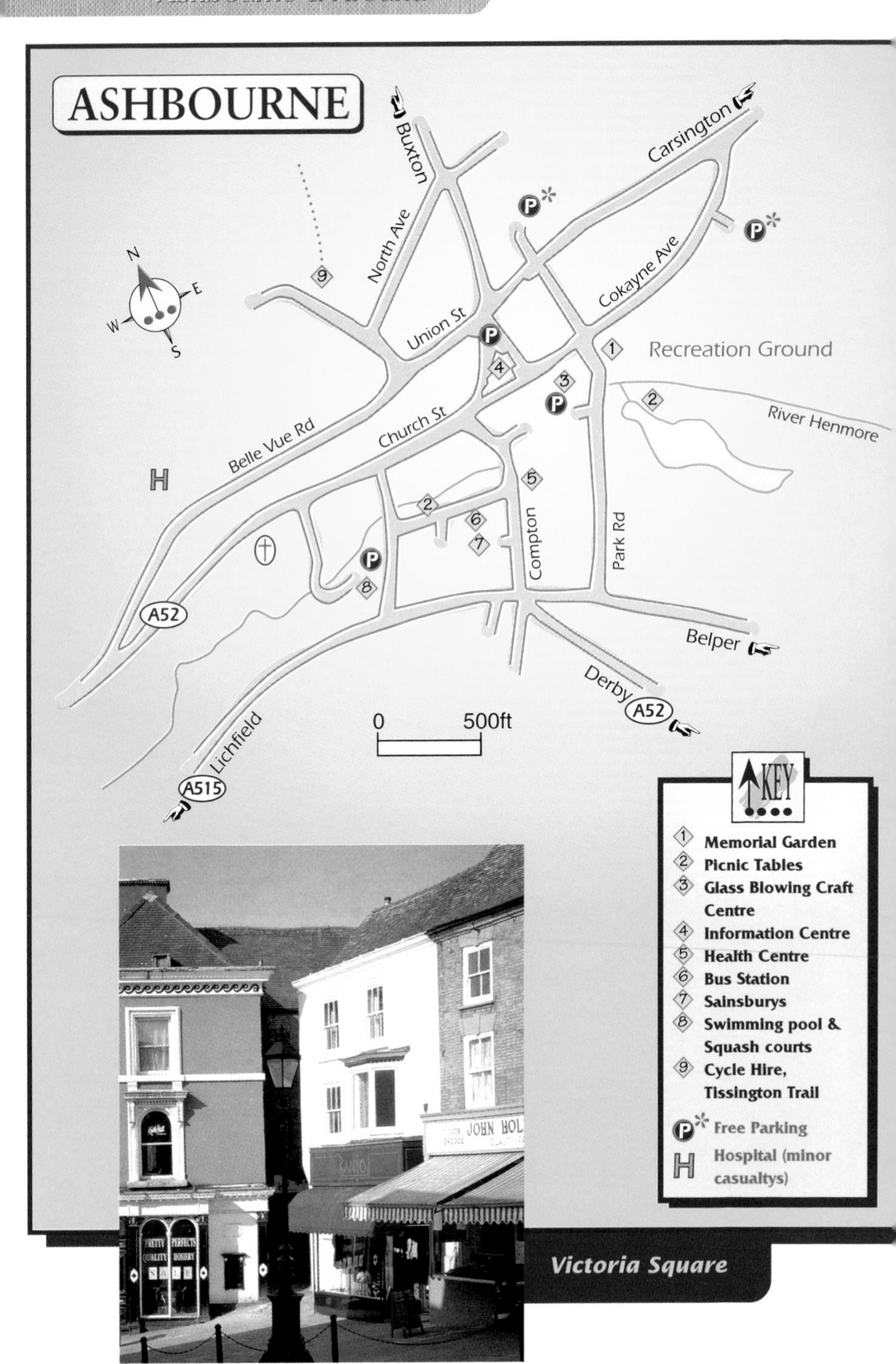

Victoria Square

St Oswald's Church

While in the street, visit **St Oswald's Church**, one of the grandest in the Peak, preferably in early spring when the churchyard is submerged beneath a carpet of daffodils. The oldest part of the existing building dates from the thirteenth century upon an earlier site, from which a Norman crypt has been located. The chancel was dedicated on the 24 April 1241. Most of the building dates from the fourteenth century. The spire rises to a height of 212ft (64m).

Derwent Crystal

Shaw Croft, Ashbourne. Demonstrations of glassblowing and decorating full English lead crystal. Factory shop ☎ 01335 345219.
Open: Monday to Saturday 9am–5pm, Sundays in summer. Demonstrations 9am–1pm only.

The alabaster monuments in the church are especially notable, as well as a fine carving in marble of Penelope Boothby. A guide book is available about the church.

There are free carparks at the Cattle Market and at Boothby Meadows, both on the outskirts of the town centre.

• VILLAGES AROUND ASHBOURNE •

Although few of the villages in the area have individual buildings of outstanding architectural merit, many are worth visiting. They are all villages which have enjoyed the patronage of some particular family. What does make them of interest is the variation of vernacular architecture, reflecting changing tastes and different building stones. Working northwards from Ashbourne, the most interesting villages are described briefly below.

Fenny Bentley lies a little way up the A515 Buxton road from Ashbourne. In the church is a curious tomb to Thomas Beresford who fought at Agincourt. The effigies of both Thomas and his wife are depicted bundled up in shrouds, as are their 21 children around the sides of the tomb. The tower of their fortified and moated manor house may be seen from the A515.

From Fenny Bentley the A515 climbs uphill where the road into Tissington can be taken to the right through a set of stone gate posts. Beyond is an avenue of lime trees, originally planted in 1815, commemorate the Battle of Waterloo. They were replaced at the end of the nineteenth century after a number blew down in a storm in 1894. The present avenue was planted in 1970.

Tissington village is worth a visit at any time. **Tissington Hall**, a large and very fine Jacobean mansion, is a popular subject for photographers, along with the wells and village pond, while the old railway station site is an access point for the Tissington Trail.

Tissington Hall

Home of the FitzHerbert family for over 400 years. Guided tours only but unrestricted access to the gardens. Refreshments ☎ 01335 390246.
Open: Monday, Tuesday and Wednesday in June and July, 2–5pm. Group visits by arrangement at other times of the year.

A visit to the village on, or just after, Ascension Day to see the annual well-dressing ceremony should not be missed. Although well-dressing now takes place in many Peakland villages throughout the summer, the ceremony at Tissington is the most well known. Here five wells (plus a children's well) are 'dressed' to depict varying religious themes.

North west of Tissington is **Alstonfield**, with a turning off the A515 opposite the New Inns Hotel, now run by Holiday Fellowship. The village is situated on the limestone plateau, with many solid buildings closely knit together. The church contains seventeenth century pews, a double-decker pulpit and a chest about 3m (10ft) long probably 700 years old. Part of the building is Norman. A guide book is available in the church (and also at Hartington Church). In the village there is a shop and café plus a pub, the George Inn, well known to ramblers and tourists. Next to the pub is the gallery of Jean Goodwin, a local artist who paints chiefly in watercolours (☎ 01335 310362 for opening times).

From Alstonfield the road to Wetton descends down to Hope Dale. On the right is the **Hope House Costume Museum and Restoration Workshop**, which opened in June 1997. Run by Notty Hornblower, the museum centres around Notty's extensive collection of some 300 costumes and 500 accessories.

Hope House Costume Museum & Restoration Workshop

Alstonfield. By appointment only. Visitors can see clothes being restored in the workshop together with a display of costumes and accessories covering the period between 1840 and the 1970s ☎ 01335 310318.

Ilam

Ilam village was rebuilt away from the Tudor Gothic style hall in the early years of the nineteenth century. The hall was built for Mr Jesse Watts-Russell between 1821 and 1826, to the design of John Shaw, as a spectacular mansion with towers and turrets. The formal buildings of **Ilam Hall** were demolished in 1935 and the remaining portion is now a youth hostel, and not open to the public.

Ilam Hall, **Ilam church** and the village school are all of interest. The view from the terrace is magnificent and it is easy to see why Ilam Hall was built on this particular site. There are two Saxon crosses in the churchyard and inside the church is the tomb of St Bertram and Sir Francis Chantrey's statue of David Pike-Watts dated 1826. Notice the former Saxon doorway to the right of the porch. The former is very fine indeed and shows Jesse Watts-Russell's father-in-law on his deathbed with his daughter and grandchildren at his bedside. The cross in the village near the bridge is dedicated to the daughter, Watts-Russell's wife, Mary.

5 miles north-west of Ashbourne. 84 acres of parkland on the banks of the River Manifold. Information centre with information on Ilam and the South Peak Estate, National Trust shop and tearoom ☎ 01335 350245. Shop open: daily April to October 11am–5pm. Other weekends 11am–4pm (excluding Christmas and New Year). Tearoom: mid-May to end-September, Friday to Tuesday 11am–5pm, winter weekends 11am–4pm.

Also worth exploring are the paths in the wood in the grounds of the hall. One leads to a grotto where William Congreve wrote the *Old Bachelor* — his stone desk and seat are still there. The path along the valley bottom known as Paradise Walk takes one past the resurgent waters of the Manifold and Hamps. Further on it passes the 'Battle Cross' found when the village was remodelled.

The riverside walk takes you past the 'boil holes'. The first and larger one is where the River Manifold can be seen rising after its underground journey from Wetton Mill. The second and smaller boil hole contains the waters of the River Hamps. Other boil holes exist nearby where other watercourses return to the surface.

The path continues on to the Riverside Lodge, where you join the Ilam to Castern Road. The last section is private and sometimes a small toll is levied.

In the grounds of the hall, **St Bertram's Bridge** gracefully spans the river. This was the old road into the village until the houses were moved away from the hall and church.

Shrovetide Football

Ashbourne is famed for its Shrovetide football match which occurs on Shrove Tuesday and Ash Wednesday. The ball is thrown up at 2pm in Shaw Croft car park behind the Green Man Inn and the game can continue until 10pm. The highly decorated ball is made of leather filled with cork. The goals are 3 miles apart on the sites of the old Clifton and Sturston Mills and teams, consisting of hundreds, are known as the 'Up'ards' and 'Down'ards'.

The rules are few and the town's shops are boarded up for safety; even the river is part of the game. It is the object of each team to get the ball back to its own goal. It is a slow-moving game and rarely are more than two goals scored in a day's play. Ashbourne's game is the last Shrovetide mass football game to be played through the streets of mainland Britain. It has survived several attempts in the nineteenth century to close it down.

The game was also played in Derby, where it was stopped in 1846. This is the origin of the expression 'a Derby game', when two local teams play each other. It is quite a local honour to turn up, or start, the game or to goal the ball. The goaler keeps the ball or, in the event of no goal, it is given to the turner-up.

The Shrovetide football "hug" with the ball outside the Health Centre

Well Dressing

Many Derbyshire villages owe their location to a reliable flow of pure water. Springs are especially important on the limestone plateau, where water quickly seeps into cracks in the rock. A regular flow was of particular importance during periods of drought or pestilence, with the plague being prevalent in the area from medieval times to the seventeenth century. Tissington's wells are reputed to have maintained their purity during an outbreak of plague in 1348-9.

"An angel appears to Mary" Hall Well, Tissington

Thus the custom of 'dressing' or adorning village wells with flowers may have originated as thanks for the supply of pure water. The custom has been practised for over 300 years, as a visitor to Staffordshire in 1680 noted that 'They have also a custom in this county ... of adorning their wells with boughs and flowers' and that the custom was associated with 'cakes, ale and a little music and dancing'.

Today the wells are decorated with flower petals pressed into clay held in a wooden framework. It is a difficult task that combines hard work with artistic skill. The clay must be cleaned of impurities before being made into the consistency of plaster. The frames must be soaked (perhaps in the village pond, as at Tissington) to prevent the clay from drying out. The design is sketched on to the wet clay, and then flower petals, berries, moss, lichen, seeds and cones are pressed into the surface. The collecting of the flowers and their application must all be done at the last minute to keep the display looking as fresh as possible.

The custom is now carried on in many villages in and around the Peak District, throughout the spring and summer. With its five wells, Tissington is the best known, while Hartington is one of the most recent to start the tradition. A full list of villages which dress their wells is given in the Fact File.

5 The Southern Limestone Plateau

Much of the limestone district of the Peak lies south of Buxton, bounded to the west by the Dove and Manifold Valleys and to the east by the River Derwent. East of Buxton, the River Wye dissects the limestone as it flows to join the Derwent. The district bounded by these valleys is a flattish plateau with interlocking stone walls forming a grey patchwork on a green quilt. Occasionally the relief is augmented by clumps of trees or sometimes long lines of trees growing along the old lead mine veins and providing shelter from the penetrating winter wind.

Dotted over the landscape are countless farms, some in small clusters and, less frequently, some grouped together in villages. It is almost a pattern for the district to see the ribbon development of the last two and a half centuries now welded into neat little villages. A good example of the linear pattern can be seen at Youlgreave and is met again in Sheldon, Chelmorton, Taddington, Elton, Bonsall, Winster and Wensley among others.

Unexpected treasures

This is an area which the motorist seems intent on passing through as he rushes between the tourist centres that surround it. It is, however, worthwhile seeking out its treasures, whether it be the dales of the Lathkill and Bradford, buildings such as Youlgreave Church and Winster Market Hall, or the archaeological remains such as Arbor Low stone circle and the smaller circles on Stanton Moor.

Prehistoric burial sites

Despite the presence of limestone, the number of caves is surprisingly small, Lathkill Head Cave being the only one of any size. Early man therefore made use of the surface of the area for burial purposes and numerous tumuli can be found marked on the OS map. It is little wonder that Thomas Bateman, the nineteenth-century barrow-digger, lived in this district, at Middleton-by-Youlgreave; few of these 'lows', as they are called, escaped his attention. The most fascinating, and of national importance, is **Arbor Low.**

Arbor Low

Situated south of Monyash and just off the Youlgreave to Parsley Hay road. Now in the care of English Heritage, this huge stone circle consists of a ring of stones surrounded by a bank and ditch, the external diameter being nearly 300ft (92m). It is considered that the stones originally stood upright, although all but one have fallen, and that there were originally 39 of them. Open all year at all reasonable times.

Adjacent to it is Gib Hill with an earlier henge. A Roman road runs just to the west of Gib Hill and an old trackway can be traced between the two. It would seem that the Roman surveyor made use of an already existing prehistoric trackway.

Stanton Moor, to the east, has an impressive collection of five stone circles and over seventy tumuli. The most celebrated circle is the one known as the **Nine Ladies**, which is not really a stone circle but the remains of a large barrow with the earth removed. The nine stones still stand, with a further stone, the King Stone, situated some 130ft (40m) away. Many of these burial mounds and circles have been excavated and an impressive collection of artifacts, created by the late J. P Heathcote and his father, may be seen at Sheffield Museum.

Above: The River Lathkill near Raper Lodge
Right: Cork Stone, Stanton Moor

To the west on **Harthill Moor** lies another circle, Nine Stones, although only four stones now survive, together with the remains of an Iron Age fort by Harthill Moor Farm. Nearby, a curious outcrop is known as **Robin Hood's Stride**; the rocks contain a small cave used as a shelter by a hermit in medieval times. It has a crucifix carved on the wall and a niche for a candle.

A fine Anglo-Saxon artifact was found in the Benty Grange tumulus, just north-west of Arbor Low. Here, Thomas Bateman uncovered the burial of a warrior together with his helmet consisting of iron straps with a silver cross fixed to the noseguard and surmounted by a bronze boar.

To the south of Middleton, beyond the Newhaven to Via Gellia road, there is an archaeological trail centred on **Roystone Grange**, after which the trail is named.

Roystone Grange Archaeological Trail

Starts at the Minninglow car park (by the old railway bridge over the Parwich to Pikehall road) and gives a fascinating insight into the area's history. It incorporates the old railway, a nineteenth-century brick kiln, the medieval Roystone Grange and an adjacent Roman farmhouse and field system. A leaflet on the trail is available from the National Park office at Bakewell.

• LATHKILL & BRADFORD DALES •

The area covered by this chapter includes Lathkill Dale and Bradford Dale, two of the most picturesque dales imaginable. The clear waters in themselves are a striking attraction, particularly when one has the time to watch the trout as they dart about. Lathkill Dale starts in an unpromising sort of way, half a mile to the east of Monyash.

Lathkill Dale

A footpath leaves the B5055 at the bottom of Bagshaw Dale and heads south-east towards Lathkill Dale. It is a convenient place to park the car. Soon, small outcrops of limestone give way to a narrow, deep and steep sided valley, devoid of water and with a rocky floor. After about a mile (1.6km) the river can usually be seen flowing from the mouth of a large cave on the right known as Lathkill Head Cave. Despite its promising entrance it is in fact a very low cave inside for a considerable distance before passages lead down to other levels. It is also dangerous in showery weather as it is prone to flood quickly.

Further downstream, at the foot of the dry valley leading up to Haddon Grove, lie the remains of Carter's Mill. This small cornmill was intact during World War II but now only the foundations survive. Here, the valley becomes wooded and the path follows the river amid leafy glades and old lead mining ruins.

Nature Reserve

Lower downstream, a water channel crossed over the valley on an aqueduct with limestone piers which have been preserved in various stages of completeness. This brought the leat to the northern side of the river where it ran to Mandale lead mine. Part of the engine house remains here, together with its associated pumping shaft which also had a waterwheel for pumping purposes. Much of the valley is part of the **Derbyshire Dales National Nature Reserve.** It is a sensitive area and visitors should not stray from the footpath. Leaflets about the reserve are available near Lathkill Lodge.

A few minute's walk from here is Lathkill Lodge with a mill pond and a former cornmill. Around the Lodge area the river bed is sometimes dry which spoils the river's attractiveness. Down-stream, a succession of eleven weirs creates a marvellous sight when you look back at them.

From the Lodge one may climb out of the valley to **Over Haddon** where there is a craft centre, or southwards up the track and across the fields to Meadow Place Grange and Youlgreave.

Lathkill Dale Craft Centre

Manor Farm, Over Haddon. Eight workshops including ceramics, furniture, clocks, stained glass, art, bookbinding and gift shop and tearoom. Facilities for the disabled
☎ 01629 812390.
Open: daily 10am-5pm. Courtyard tearoom open as shops except January-March, weekends only.

Nearby is The Lathkill, a lovely pub with memorable views down into Lathkill Dale and beyond to Youlgreave and Stanton Moor. It has a large restaurant and bar food. At the top end of Lathkill Dale, food is available at The Bull's Head in Monyash.

Ancient bridges

At **Conksbury**, the old packhorse bridge carrying the Bakewell to Youlgreave road is crossed before continuing down the opposite bank towards Raper Lodge. Surprisingly unmentioned by Pevsner, this handsome house looks down on the river and another old packhorse bridge.

The river meadows soon lead to **Alport** with its seventeenth and eighteenth century cottages, ancient bridge, and another mill and mill pool in an idyllic setting. Nearby the Lathkill meets the Bradford and closely hugs the road before meeting the River Wye at Picory Corner.

Bradford Dale

The River Bradford commences south of **Middleton-by-Youlgreave**, but the dale only becomes of consequence at Middleton where a track leads down to the dale. The track is a little rough underfoot and the bare limestone outcrops and overhanging trees give nothing away of the beauty of the dale beyond, as it brings one down to an old pumping station. The beauty of **Bradford Dale** lies in the six pools of crystal-clear water reflecting the mature trees which line the sides of this steep-sided dale at its upper end, downstream of the old pumping station. The track between Middleton and the river is a mass of yellow celandines in spring.

Youlgreave spills down into the dale, but the intrusion is on the whole a sympathetic one. A clapper bridge enables one to cross the river and either proceed downstream or walk up to the village. Beyond the bridge, the path hugs the river until a road crosses the valley, which by now is getting much more shallow and open. Just beyond the road a bridge crosses the river yet again and a path follows the river down to Alport.

Youlgreave is typical of the Peak District linear villages with its sturdy church displaying architecture spanning 800 years, standing in a dominating position at the end of the main street. It too was an important lead mining village and its many houses are old workers' cottages.

The old Co-op, also featured in *The Virgin and the Gypsy*, is now a youth hostel. It is situated opposite a large, round stone tank dated 1829 known as The Fountain. Youlgreave still had until 1998 its own water supply from Bradford Dale and the tank is a reminder of when it was first installed. It has a capacity of 1,200 gallons, but is no longer used. Further down the main street to the west is the old hall, adjacent to the road.

Upland Villages

In addition to the dales there are many villages scattered throughout the area, chiefly in a linear pattern on the limestone plateau. In the north, one such is **Chelmorton** an interesting place to explore. The oldest part of the village was obviously near to the hill and its spring, which is why the church and pub now appear to be at the end of a cul-de-sac. With the coming of the first enclosure, land appears to have been allotted so that each cottage had a few strips behind it and this order has been preserved, so that even today there are many narrow fields stretching away; later enclosures resorted to a more regular pattern.

Monyash & Winster

To the south-west lies **Monyash**. It was once an important centre of the lead mining industry, with a weekly market. The old market cross still stands on the green, its base supposedly made from the old village stocks. Of the four former village ponds (or 'meres') at Monyash, only Fere Mere remains.

To the south lies **Winster**, with a similar history of dependence on lead mining. Look for the **Market House** in the centre of the village, which was described by Pevsner as being of the fifteenth or sixteenth century, although its original open ground floor arches have been built in with brick to give it more stability. In the main street lies the early Georgian Hall, now a hotel.

Monyash church & Fere Mere

Winster Market House

First property acquired by the National Trust in Derbyshire. Small information room ☎ 01335 350245. Open: daily, end of March to end of Ocotber.

Other Attractions

If you are travelling along the lane to Winster from Birchover, look out for the restored village stocks. Above the village is the old village quarry. It is still in production, supplying cut gritstone to local builders (who are often required to build in traditional materials) plus markets further afield.

Depending on time available, a drive around some of Winster's neighbouring villages should not be overlooked. There are some delightful corners to be seen in **Stanton-in-the-Peak**, just to the north. It has an unusually named pub, *The Flying Childers*, named after a horse belonging to The Duke of Devonshire, purchased in 1719. Look out for the Cork Stone, Cat Stone and Andle Stone on Stanton Moor — huge natural blocks of gritstone, the latter having foot-holes and iron handles for climbing to the top. More obvious is the Earl Grey Tower, built in 1832 to celebrate the passing of the Reform Bill.

The area now under discussion contains some of the deepest and formerly the richest lead mines in the Peak. The most notable remains are those of **Magpie Mine** near to **Sheldon.** They can be seen from the Monyash to Ashford-in-the-Water road.

Magpie Mine

Near Sheldon. Impressive mine buildings and winding gear. The site is open to visitors, but cars should be left on the road and all shafts avoided. Details of access and guidebook can be obtained from the Peak District Mining Museum at Matlock Bath ☎ 01629 583834. Open at all times as footpath crosses the site.

Magpie owes its survival to its use as a lead mine until the post-war years; it finally closed in 1958. Today, when viewed from the nearby road, it looks an impressive sight with its huge engine-house, head-gear (supporting the cage), two chimney stacks and other buildings, including a cottage. The mine-drawing shaft is 728ft (222m) deep and many other shafts exist on the vein, or rake, which passes through the site.

All shafts should be avoided for safety.

This large and complex site has an interesting history despite the fact that the lead ore extracted was not great.

Between Middleton-by-Wirksworth and Bolehill is the **National Stone Centre**. Situated on a 50 acre (20 hectares) site, there is a 'Story of Stone' exhibition from pre-historic times to the present and a Fossil Trail amid a site of special scientific interest.

National Stone Centre

Porter Lane, Wirksworth. Exhibition, shop with a large selection of minerals, fossils and gemstones for sale, refreshments ☎ 01629 825403. Open: daily all year, October to March 10am–4pm; Easter to October 10am–5pm.

Off the Cromford to Wirksworth road at Bolehill is the Black Rocks Trail. There are three woodland trails around the **Black Rocks** outcrop, a picnic area plus a walk on the High Peak Trail. The gritstone rocks here are popular with rock climbers. Following the High Peak Trail to the west for about a mile leads to **Middleton Top Engine House** built to enable the hauling of waggons up a steep 1:8.75 incline on the Cromford and High Peak Railway.

Middleton Top Engine House

Middleton Top, Wirksworth. Signposted off the B5036 Cromford to Wirksworth road. Engine working on 1st weekend in each month and Bank Holiday Mondays.
☎ 01629 823204.
Open: Easter to October, 10.30am-5pm.

Just north of **Middleton-by-Wirksworth** on the A5012 Cromford-Newhaven road is Good Luck lead mine, which has been turned into a mine museum. Although it is still being explored and old passages dug out, a lot of workings may be seen. The passage is narrow in places, low in others, giving a good impression of a typical lead mine of the area.

Good Luck Mine

Via Gellia, SK270565.
A typical small lead mine. Details from Peak District Mining Museum, Matlock Bath ☎ 01629 583834.
Open: first Sunday in every month. Park in layby upstream and opposite the Tufa Cottage.

Wirksworth

To the south of the region lies **Wirksworth.** It would be easy to dismiss it as a drab town set amid the devastation of centuries of mining and quarrying. However there has been much conservation work here in recent years and there are several interesting buildings which should be sought out. The church is hidden behind the shops, having access from several narrow passages. The church contains a richly carved stone coffin lid of about AD800, found under the floor in 1820. Even though incomplete it depicts forty figures and is regarded as one of the most interesting early Anglo-Saxon remains in Britain. The church-

Town Hall, Wirksworth

yard is circular in shape — an indication of a very early Christian settlement.

A path circles the churchyard creating a backwater of peace and quiet. Walk around the north side of the church past the old Grammar School, founded in 1576 and rebuilt in 1828 in a neo-Gothic style. Its battlements and pinnacles create a pleasing elevation. It is now used for furniture manufacture.

Near the top of Coldwell Street, towards the Market Place, a passage on the right of the United Reform Church leads into Chapel Lane. On the left, some 200yd (185m) or so up the lane, stands the **Moot Hall** which was rebuilt in 1814. It still houses the standard measure for lead ore — a bronze dish made in 1513. At each sitting in this building of the Barmoot Court, the jury members receive tobacco to smoke after their meal. Britain's oldest industrial court still purchases clay pipes for its members to smoke their tobacco!

Near the town centre is a **heritage centre** where local customs and industries are explained, along with other aspects of the town. It has various exhibits: the Quarryman's House Place which illustrates the lifestyle of a quarryman a century ago; the local customs of well dressing and clypping the church are explained together with features on local quarrying and leadmining.

Wirksworth Heritage Centre

Crown Yard. Situated in the old silk and velvet mill, staffed by volunteers. Local customs and industries explained. Computer game describes historic Wirksworth. Restaurant and craft workshops ☎ 01629 825225. Open: Easter to mid-July, end of September to end of October 10.30am–4.40pm, Tuesday to Saturday and Bank Holidays, other Sundays 1–4.30pm. Mid-July to end of September open daily 10am-5pm. Some opening November to March.

To the west of Wirksworth is **Carsington Reservoir**, opened by HM the Queen in 1992. There is plenty to see and do at Carsington Water, in fact it is sensible to allow a full day.

As you enter the Visitor Centre, look closely at the bulletins posted by the door — they include factual information on how much water is in the reservoir. In the summer of 1996 it was only 39per cent full. The reservoir is a popular spot for bird watching with Carsington Bird Club and several hides along the trails which surround the water. The paths are well waymarked and regularly used by ramblers and cyclists and there are plenty of picnic tables and a childrens' play area near the centre. Look out for special events, especially the Country Fair in the autumn.

6 Cromford & the Matlocks

North of Wirksworth in the Derwent Valley lies Cromford, which grew as a result of the prosperous mills of Sir Richard Arkwright. Arkwright built the Greyhound Inn together with houses for his workers and a school for their children. On the south side of the road to Wirksworth, North Street was built by him and the school is situated at the end of the street. Behind the Wirksworth road and just to the east of North Street is the village lock up and the 'tail' or beginning of Cromford Sough. The mine water is piped across the A6 and was used to supply water to Arkwright's Mill, crossing Mill Lane on a cast iron aqueduct dated 1821, and to the Cromford Canal. The mill is being developed as a museum and a tour guide is available to describe the various features of this historically important mill.

Arkwright's Mill

Mill Lane. On minor road leading to Lea and Holloway, 200yd (185m) east of Cromford crossroads on A6. The world's first successful water-powered cotton spinning mill. Exhibitions, audio-visual display, shop and café
☎ 01629 824297.
Open: daily 9.30am-5pm, closed Christmas Day.

It was at **Cromford** that Sir Richard Arkwright established the world's first water powered cotton mill in 1772, plus Masson Mill built in 1783, situated alongside the A6 between Cromford and Matlock Bath. The latter still proudly displays the legend 'Sir Richard Arkwright & Co, Established 1769'.

From the Cromford Canal Wharf there is a pleasant towpath which leads to **High Peak Wharf** with its buildings from the Cromford and High Peak Railway. Vehicle access can be made to a car park from off the Cromford to Lea road, where the latter turns to the left away from

Below: Cromford Church

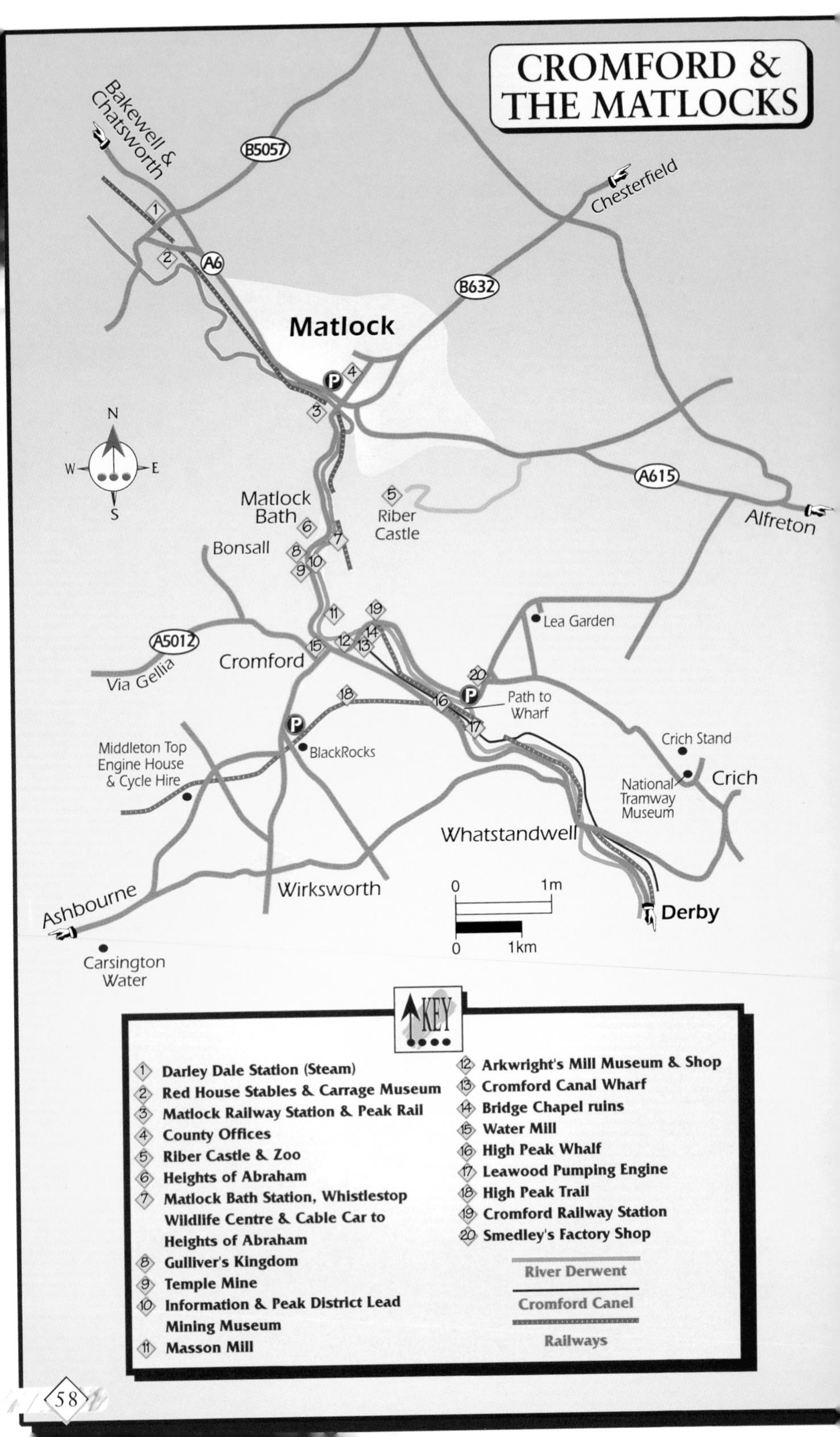
CROMFORD & THE MATLOCKS
Bakewell & Chatsworth
B5057
Chesterfield
A6
B632
Matlock
N
W
E
S
Matlock Bath
Riber Castle
Bonsall
A615
Alfreton
Lea Garden
A5012
Via Gellia
Cromford
Path to Wharf
Crich Stand
Middleton Top Engine House & Cycle Hire
BlackRocks
National Tramway Museum
Crich
Whatstandwell
Wirksworth
0
1m
0
1km
Derby
Ashbourne
Carsington Water
KEY
1 Darley Dale Station (Steam)
2 Red House Stables & Carrage Museum
3 Matlock Railway Station & Peak Rail
4 County Offices
5 Riber Castle & Zoo
6 Heights of Abraham
7 Matlock Bath Station, Whistlestop Wildlife Centre & Cable Car to Heights of Abraham
8 Gulliver's Kingdom
9 Temple Mine
10 Information & Peak District Lead Mining Museum
11 Masson Mill
12 Arkwright's Mill Museum & Shop
13 Cromford Canal Wharf
14 Bridge Chapel ruins
15 Water Mill
16 High Peak Whalf
17 Leawood Pumping Engine
18 High Peak Trail
19 Cromford Railway Station
20 Smedley's Factory Shop
River Derwent
Cromford Canel
Railways

the Derwent Valley. A path crosses the river and runs adjacent to a sewage works to reach the canal, wharf and the Leawood Pumping Station.

High Peak Junction Workshops

High Peak Junction, Nr Cromford. Signposted off A6 in Cromford. Restored railway workshops of Cromford and High Peak railways. Display, video, model working forge, shop ☎ 01629 822831. Open: Easter to October, weekends and Bank Holidays; June to mid-September daily 10.30am–5pm. Winter Saturdays and Sundays 10.30am–4pm.

Leawood Pumping Station

Cromford canal towpath, off Cromford to Crich road. 1849 beam engine, fully restored and steamed periodically. Enquiries to Leawood Pumphouse, c/o Middleton Top Visitor Centre, Wirksworth, Matlock ☎ 01629 823204.

When the rhododendrons are in flower in May and June it is worth visiting **Lea Gardens**. This was an old quarry site where planting of rhododendrons and timber began over 50 years ago. The scent of the flowers pervades the whole wood and the colours of the flowers have an amazing variety and beauty. A season ticket is good value for money as the colours change throughout the summer.

Lea Gardens

Lea, nr Matlock. A rare collection of rhododendrons, azaleas, alpines and conifers in a lovely woodland setting. Plants for sale. Tea shop ☎ 01629 534380. Open: mid-March to end of July, daily 10am-7pm

A diversion of a mile or so leads to the outskirts of **Crich** and the **Tramway Museum** with its national collection of trams. They vary from a horse-drawn Sheffield tram of 1874 to another Sheffield tram of 1950, which was the last one in the city when the service finished in 1960. The car park ticket entitles you to ride on the selection of trams operated on a mile of track down the edge of a quarry. Above, the quarry is dominated by Crich Stand — a monument to the Sherwood Foresters who fell in the two World Wars. When you take your tram ride, look out for the lead mining display erected by the Peak District Mines Historical Society. You can get off to look at this and take another tram back.

National Tramway Museum

Crich, Nr Matlock. Unlimited rides on 12 miles (2.4km) of tram tracks. Braille guide books are available and there are wheelchair ramps, although the design of the old trams preclude the access of wheelchairs ☎ 01773 852565. Open: June to September daily, April, May and October Saturday to Thursday, 10am–5.30pm. Open from Easter if earlier.

Peak District Mining Museum & Temple Mine

The Pavilion, Matlock Bath. Trevithick's giant water pressure engine. Climbing shafts and tunnels. Displays of geology, minerals and mining in the Peak District since Roman times. Visit Temple Mine to experience an early 20th century lead and fluorspar mine. Shop selling souvenirs, specialist mining books and local interest books ☎ 01629 583834. Open: daily except 25 December, 11am–4pm (later closing in summer).

Upriver from Cromford is **Matlock Bath**, a mecca for many visitors to this area. Full of hustle and bustle, crowds and souvenir shops, it is perhaps not for those who come to the Peak District for the beauty and peace of its hills and dales. The A6 becomes choked with cars on sunny Bank Holidays. Not surprisingly, there is much to see, so allow plenty of time and a full wallet. One of the more recent additions is the **Mining Museum**, run by the Peak District Mines Historical Society. The centrepiece of its exhibits is a huge water-pressure engine found in a mine at Winster. This is an interesting, not a stuffy museum, and while you follow the exhibits, children can explore simulated passages and shafts.

A dramatic addition to the attractions at Matlock Bath opened at Easter 1984. Now visitors can take a cable car ride up to the **Heights of Abraham**, which gives a spectacular and unique view of the Derwent Valley. The cable car station is a little upstream of Matlock Bath Railway Station. It is easy to locate by looking for the cables slung over the A6 and the River Derwent.

There is a good range of shops, a promenade above the river and a railway station. Each year, Matlock Bath has its illuminations with illuminated floats on the river and a firework display. More details on dates can be obtained from the information office next to the Mining Museum.

A further new addition to the attractions here is the **Whistlestop**

• Attractions •

Heights of Abraham

Cable cars, caverns and country park. Victoria Prospect Tower, Show Caverns, Owl Maze, Explorer's Challenge and Nature Trail. Coffee shop, restaurant and gift shop ☎ 01629 582365. Open: daily from Easter to end of October, 10am–5pm, later in high season.

Elsewhere in the town there is **Gulliver's Kingdom** for young children, and there are several show caves and mines.

Cable cars, Heights of Abraham

Gulliver's Kingdom

Temple Walk Turn up the hill to the south of and opposite the Pavilion. Theme park for young families. Royal Cave, adjacent to Gulliver's Kingdom and only accessible on an inclusive ticket from there ☎ 01629 580540. Open: daily, Easter to October, 10.30am–5.30pm available. Party rates available. Staff help available for wheelchairs on the slopes.

Matlock Bath Aquarium

North Parade. Matlock Bath. Aquaria, hologram gallery, petrifying well and gemstone collection ☎ 01629 583624.
Open: daily Easter to end of September 10am–5.30pm. Winter, weekends only.

Visitor Centre, in some of the old railway buildings (built in 1849 in a Swiss Chalet style) adjacent to the station. The main former Midland Railway station building is now a gift shop and the old goods building has been converted to an educational centre.

Whistlestop Countryside Centre

Old Railway Station, Matlock Bath. Wildlife gift shop incorporating exhibition on the Derbyshire Wildlife Trust ☎ 01629 580958. Open: daily April to October, 10am–5pm. Winter Saturday and Sunday 12noon–4pm.

On a similar theme is the **Riber Castle Wildlife Park**, established in the grounds of the mock castle which dominates the skyline south of Matlock.

Riber Castle Wildlife Park

Situated off A615 at Tansley, via Alders Lane, 1 mile (1.6km) to Riber. World famous Lynx collection; home of rare breeds and endangered species. Caféteria, picnic areas, gift shop. Magnificent views over Derwent Valley. Licensed bar ☎ 01629 582073. Open: daily from 10am (closed 25 December)

Riber Castle

High Tor

Access from near Matlock Bath station, Church Street or Dale Road, Matlock or from Starkholmes. Explore old Roman lead workings, woodland walks, children's playground and café. Open: daily, 10am–dusk

Upstream from Matlock Bath railway station are the **High Tor Grounds** — 60 acres (24 hectares) in extent with walks and views down into the Derwent Valley, with the river nearly 400ft (123m) below. Access is from Dale Road or Church Street, Matlock, or just upriver from Matlock Bath railway station.

A little south of Matlock Bath is the **New Bath Hotel.** Most people tend to regard it as being purely residential, but this is not so. When you begin to flag a little in Matlock Bath, it is an excellent choice for coffee and biscuits. **Matlock** itself is a good shopping centre, but it lacks the architectural appeal for example of Buxton, Bakewell or Ashbourne. Fortunately its shops are on the flat, for much of the town itself overlooks the river.

Abbey Brook Cactus Nursery

Old Hackney Lane, Matlock. Over 2,000 different species of cacti and succulents on display and for sale. Tearoom available at Robert Young's adjacent nursery.
☎ 01629 580306.
Open: Monday to Saturday 1–5pm, Sunday 12noon–5pm.

Matlock

An unusual attraction in Matlock is the **Abbey Brook Cactus Nursery**. It is the leading supplier to garden centres in the United Kingdom. There are a fascinating variety of cacti of which many are scented and some display unusually large flowers. Entry to the show house of giant cacti is free. Going towards Bakewell from Matlock the nursery is situated near the Whitworth Hospital. Turn off the A6 by Robert Young's Garden Centre or Old Hackney Lane.

Matlock developed as a spa town and many hydros, or more correctly hydropathic establishments, were built in the mid-nineteenth century. The last major hydro to survive was Smedleys, which finally closed its doors in 1955. It is a massive structure and is worth having a look at. It is now the County Council Offices and was built by John Smedley, who also built Riber Castle. Matlock formerly had a tramway and a couple of trams used to run up and down the steep hill (Bank Road) between the Crown Square roundabout and Smedley's Hydro.

Between Matlock and Rowsley are two museums, both with a transport theme. The Peak Rail Society has a centre at Darley Dale Station (see chapter 8) and nearby is the **Red House Stables Carriage Museum.** Here one may browse around one of the country's finest collections of horse-drawn vehicles. The museum offers scenic tours by coach and four-in-hand, plus driving tuition for which prior booking is needed.

Red House Stables Carriage Museum

Darley Dale. Over forty horse-drawn vehicles, equipment and harness rooms.
☎ 01629 733583.
Open: daily from 10am.

7 Buxton & the Northern Limestone Plateau

Opposite: The Old Hall Hotel. The room occupied by Mary, Queen of Scots still survives
Below: The Palace Hotel, built 1867 – 68

The River Wye rises on Axe Edge and flows down to Buxton before turning eastwards to divide the limestone region into two. Much of its course north of Rowsley is followed by the A6 trunk road. The valley has two quite distinct features. North-west of Bakewell it is narrow and deeply incised with sheer limestone bluffs which in places even overhang the river. It is joined by many tributary valleys, mostly quite deep but chiefly devoid of water. The largest are Great Rocks Dale, the two Deep Dales, Monks Dale, Tideswell Dale, Cressbrook Dale and Taddington Dale. South-east of Bakewell, the river flows across softer, younger rocks which have eroded more easily creating a wider valley.

Fortunately, the A6 road took advantage of Taddington Dale and so spared perhaps the most beautiful part of the Wye, between Topley Pike and the bottom of Monsal Dale. Part of this can be viewed from the car, but much is preserved for the rambler, including the most interesting parts of Chee Dale, Water-cum-Jolly Dale and parts of Monsal Dale.

North of the Wye, the limestone plateau is an area of drystone walls and dry valleys with dairy and sheep farms which includes some minor hills such as Longstone Edge, Bradwell Moor and Eldon Hill. It has also been an important area for quarrying and lead mining.

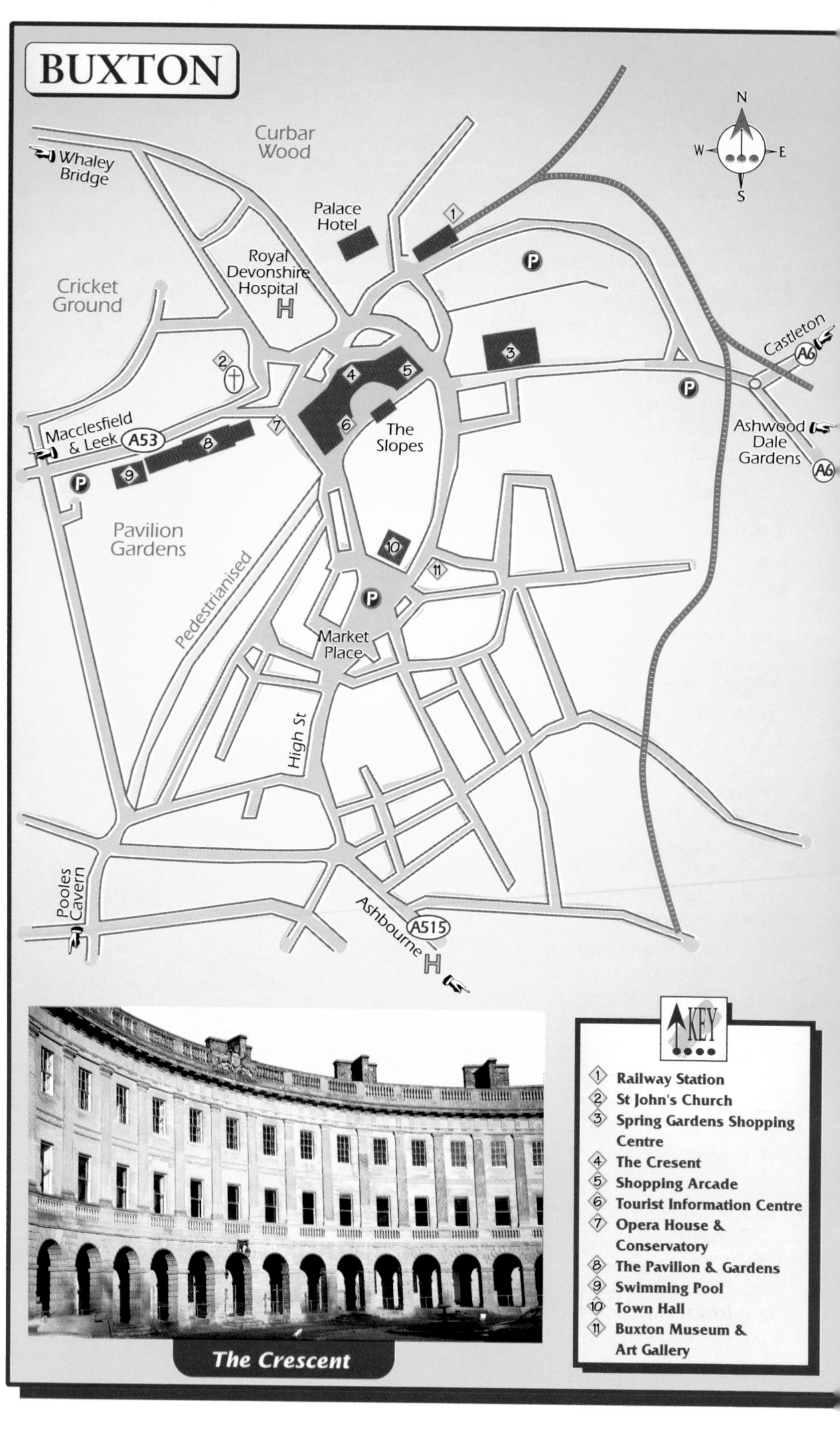

The Crescent

• BUXTON •

Buxton itself has an ancient history. It attracted the Romans because of its warm mineral water which bubbles up to the surface. They built a bath here and called their settlement *Aquae Arnemetiae*. To the bath came Roman roads from Derby, Leek, Brough (*Navio*) east of Castleton, and south from near Glossop from a fort probably called *Ardotalia* but more popularly known by the fictitious *Melandra*. Other roads came from the west and the north-west. A Roman milestone found in 1856 is now preserved in the museum.

After the Romans left, the spring was not entirely forgotten and by Tudor times it had a reputation for curing invalids. Mary Queen of Scots whilst a prisoner in the custody of William, Earl of Shrewsbury, came here to seek relief from rheumatism. The spa waters rise from underground at a temperature of 82 degrees Fahrenheit.

The Crescent built adjacent to the spring was designed by John Carr of York for the fifth Duke of Devonshire. It was built between 1780 and 1790 and was the first important imitation of the Royal Crescent at Bath, as part of a deliberate plan by the Duke to build Buxton into a spa town to rival that city. It was built primarily as a hotel and shopping complex and was partly occupied from 1786. At the north end was the Great Hotel, until 1993 the public library.

Adjoining the Crescent were the thermal and natural baths; the latter at the south end and the former at the northern end. The thermal baths have been converted into a shopping complex, retaining some features of the old baths. Behind the Crescent are **The Pavilion, Opera House** and **Pavilion Gardens**. The gardens and Conservatory are worth a visit, as is the restored Opera House, which has a high reputation for the quality of its performances.

Largest dome in the world

After the building of The Crescent, patronage by the Devonshire family continued with the building of the stables to the rear of The Crescent during 1785-90. This was converted to the **Devonshire Royal Hospital** in 1859, and the central courtyard previously used for exercising the horses was covered with a dome in 1881-2. At the time, it was the largest dome in the world, being 156ft (48m) in diameter and weighing 560 tons!

The Opera House was built in 1903 and retains its wonderful interior. It was built adjacent to The Pavilion which dates from 1871. Across the road from the Opera House, lovers of street furniture will appreciate the Victorian post box. The large concert hall next to the Pavilion was added in 1875. The entrance to the Conservatory is to the left of the main entrance to the Opera House and was refurbished in the early 1980s. The area beyond the Conservatory suffered from an arson attack and has been remodelled internally with a pleasant café on the first floor looking out over the gardens and restaurant below. Beyond the Concert Hall is a modern swimming pool and adjacent car park.

Blue John & Black Marble

There are several attractions for young children in the Pavilion Gardens, which are most attractive in the summer. Owing to the town's altitude, spring arrives late and sometimes you can see daffodils and tulips in flower in the gardens in June!

The **Buxton Museum and Art Gallery** in Terrace Road includes archaeological remains found locally and from the Manifold Valley. There are also fine examples of objects made of Blue John stone from Castleton and Black Marble from Ashford-in-the-Water. Of special note are the excellent dioramas showing life in prehistoric times — complete with sound effects. There is much else to see in Buxton. A walk along Spring Gardens, the main shopping street, is recommended. The town, one of the highest in England, has a railway station, good bus services and municipal conveniences such as the Pavilion Gardens, bowling greens and two golf clubs.

Buxton Museum & Art Gallery

Terrace Road. Extensive collections of geology, archaeology, prehistory and local history relating to the Peak District. Temporary monthly art exhibitions.
☎ 01298 24658.
Open: Tuesday to Friday 9.30am–5.30pm. Saturday 9.30am–5pm.

Off Spring Gardens, an indoor shopping centre has been developed, with a further innovative shopping complex at the former Thermal Baths adjacent to The Crescent. It gives a good idea of what the Baths must have looked like, and the original chair in which arthritic patients could be lowered into the water has been preserved. There is a café on the first floor. Despite the demise of its status as a spa town, Buxton is still a very pleasant town to visit and explore.

Poole's Cavern & Buxton Country Park

Green Lane. Beautiful natural show cave; 100 acres (40 hectares) of woodland with nature trail, free car park, picnic area, toilets and shop ☎ 01298 26978. Open: daily Easter to end of October, closed Wednesday (except high season) 10am–5pm.

South of the town, on Grin Low, is **Solomon's Temple**. This folly was built to provide labour for out-of-work men. It was restored a few years ago at a cost of £25,000 and can be reached from **Poole's Cavern** situated to the south of the town. It is worth visiting if only for the panoramic view over Buxton.

Poole's Cavern is the only show cave on the west side of the peak and is easy to walk through. It is beneath Grin Plantation, a wooded area planted on old lime ash tips. During his tour of Britain, Daniel Defoe visited Buxton and was most impressed by Poole's Cavern but, incidentally, not very impressed with the accommodation available in the town. One suspects it would be different today, for there are now numerous hotels and guest houses.

The northern portion of the limestone region has many similarities to the area south of the Wye Valley. A rolling landscape of green fields with an intricate system of dry-stone walls is synonymous with the Peak District limestone region as a whole. Other than the River Wye itself, the area is devoid of any river system. It is, of course, bounded in the east by the River Derwent.

The Devonshire Royal Hospital

• THE WYE VALLEY •

There are no counterparts for the river systems of the Dove, Manifold, Lathkill and its smaller tributary, the Bradford. The presence of several dry valleys has already been indicated and while pleasant enough, they lack the attractions that flowing water can create. The most interesting dale therefore is that of the Wye.

The Monsal Trail at Monsal Head

It is crossed by a road at Miller's Dale, there is a minor road to Litton, and a road to Cressbrook and Wardlow Mires drops into the dale at Monsal Head. A little further south, the A6 runs up the valley to the bottom of Taddington Dale and returns to it for the section between Topley Pike and Buxton. There is much to see on foot and fortunately the linear pattern of the valley can be overcome by catching a bus back to one's starting point if the need arises. Buses run between Buxton and both Tideswell (for Sheffield) and Bakewell (for Derby and Chesterfield).

Topley Pike (SK103725) offers a good place to start. One can park opposite Tarmac's quarry at this point, where a minor road turns down to the river. It is marked on the OS White Peak map. This track follows the river down to the bottom of Great Rocks Dale. The track passes through well-wooded surroundings, sharing the narrow valley with the railway which crosses three times overhead. Upon reaching the footbridge and the row of cottages — presumably built for workers of the disused quarry behind — one also leaves Wye Dale for **Chee Dale**. Below here, the dale becomes much more interesting and, in wet weather, even adventuresome!

Chee Dale

For most of the way, the path in **Chee Dale** hugs the river. In places it becomes precipitous, particularly where it runs on the south side of the river near to the railway arch, and also just upstream from the tributary Flag Dale. The valley is characterised in places by sheer limestone bluffs, several of which overhang the valley bottom. In two places, this forces the path into the river and onto stepping stones. If the river is in flood, the dale can be impassable. The outcrops of limestone, some with sheer water-worn slabs and overhangs, offer considerable sport to climbers. The valley is well-wooded in places which offers some variety of scenery.

Miller's Dale

Beyond Flag Dale, the valley opens out a little as one approaches the footbridge carrying the path from Wormhill to Blackwell over the river. Beyond here it is just a short walk into **Miller's Dale**. In former days Miller's Dale was locally an important place. It not only served as a railway station for many surrounding villages including Tideswell, but Manchester to Derby through-trains stopped here to pick up passengers from Buxton. The passenger traffic, together with the limestone traffic, made Miller's Dale a big station for its location. The Tideswell to Taddington road also crosses the valley here and river, road and railway are neighbours yet again. There are two quite impressive railway bridges situated side by side, the initial bridge being augmented in 1903 by the second one, 40 years after the line opened.

From Miller's Dale to Monsal Head

Commerce also dictated a road down the dale at this point to serve **Litton Mill**. Originally it was a waterwheel driven cotton mill, and textile manufacturing has only recently ceased. The mill earned a reputation for the unfortunate excesses of child labour in the early nineteenth century, epitomised in Walter Unsworth's novel *The Devil's Mill*. The path down the dale proceeds through the mill yard, at which point the road ends. The current mill dates from 1874 when a fire destroyed the earlier mill of 1782.

Beyond here lies **Water-cum-Jolly Dale**. One wonders whether the impounded water, backing up from Cressbrook Mill, inspired the name or whether it dates from a time prior to this. On a summer's day, the broad expanse of water with the waterworn limestone bluff behind reflecting in the millpool and the occasional duck or moorhen on the surface, adds to the tranquillity of the dale. **Cressbrook Mill** no longer operates. The main structure which dates from 1815, replaced an earlier mill built by Arkwright in 1779.

Monsal Head

Downstream from the mill the path follows the lane to **Monsal Head**. Take not the first bridge across the river, but the second, situated where the road begins to rise towards Monsal Head. The path goes through the arches that carried the railway line to Buxton from Bakewell. Ruskin stongly objected to the intrusion of the railway, but the line has mellowed into the landscape and the viewpoint from Monsal Head is now, ironically, well known and popular with photographers.

Just downstream from the railway arches the River Wye tumbles over a weir that many people must recognise from the numerous postcards and calendars in which it features. From here the path cuts through the meadows at the bottom of the wood to meet the A6 at the foot of **Taddington Dale** where there is a picnic site, car park and toilets.

Magpie Sough

Below Taddington Dale, the river meanders slowly to Ashford-in-the-Water and Bakewell. A footpath follows much of the route, passing through Great Shacklow Wood, emerging by the river close to where the water flowing down Magpie Sough reaches the Wye. The sough drains Magpie Mine, situated over a mile away south of Sheldon village.

The path is an easy walk amid a leafy glade, reaching the fields by an old watermill. There are three waterwheels here; two are attached to an old saw mill which was used to produce bobbins and wooden spindles for Sir Richard Arkwright's nearby cotton mills. A third and much smaller one was used to pump water up to Sheldon village before mains water was laid.

Ashford Black Marble

After a short walk through the fields, the path reaches Kirkdale and the road to Sheldon. The works depot at Kirkdale used to be a marble mill and many of the black marble slabs visible in Derbyshire churches were cut and polished here. The stone, really a dark limestone which takes a high polish and looks like marble, was mined from two localities nearby. The marble works lost most of its buildings when the Ashford bypass was built.

Ashford-in-the-Water is worth a look around, particularly to view the old packhorse bridge — Sheepwash Bridge — and its neighbouring pump shelter, although the village pump has now gone. The village was once at least equal in importance to Bakewell, but that has all now changed. As early as the seventeenth century, 300 packhorses, laden with malt, passed northwards through the village each week. The bypass, constructed in 1931, took away much of the traffic. The Sheepwash Bridge was built in the seventeenth century and the sheepwash remains on the far side from the village.

In the church are some paper garlands hanging in memory of girls who died unmarried. There are also some memorials in the local black marble. The mines are on either side of the valley at the western end of the village, but should not be entered.

• NORTH OF THE RIVER WYE •

The limestone region north of the River Wye is a patchwork of small villages and undulating farmland cut by deep valleys such as Cressbrook Dale, Coombs Dale and Middleton Dale. The largest village in the limestone area is Tideswell. There must be many visitors to the Peak who miss — or drive straight through — Tideswell. With its multitude of shops — including a Co-op, a chemist, two restaurants, banks and a filling station — it can satisfy most requirements of a visitor.

Tideswell

The area around the church is a pure gem. Park near the church and have a look at the **George Hotel**, a fine coaching inn with Venetian windows and dating from 1730. To the rear of the church is the vicarage and at its side, the library, a superb example of vernacular architecture combining cut blocks of limestone with gritstone quoins and mullions.

The original church was enlarged in the fourteenth century and is very impressive. It took so long to build that the architectural style started off at the east end in 'Early English' style. By the time the masons were building the west end, the 'Perpendicular' was in fashion and it was in this style that the building was finished. It certainly should be visited, and fully lives up to its title of **'Cathedral of the Peak'**.

Around Tideswell

Elsewhere the villages follow the familiar pattern, either elongated or set around a village square. Most are very small but with little features here and there that make a visit worthwhile such as the stocks in **Litton**; the fourteenth century cross and adjacent village pond in **Foolow**; and the memorial to James Brindley, the canal engineer, at **Wormhill** where he was born.

East of Litton on the road to Wardlow Mires is the top of **Cressbrook Dale**, its steep sided valley coming right up to the road. A pronounced feature of this end of the valley is Peter's Stone which is a detached block of limestone of significant size. It can be viewed from the A623 at Wardlow Mires, but the signposted footpath from there down the top of the dale enables you to get quite close.

The fourteenth century cross in Foolow. It is worth more than a passing glance. The cross was resited on the green in 1868 at the rear of a flat stone with an iron ring set in its top surface. The stone is a bull baiting stone and must be very old, for bull baiting was made illegal in 1835. The cross stands by the old village mere, fed by a spring with a wall around it. Around this centre sit the village school, manor house, pub, chapel and other old village buildings dating from the seventeenth and eighteenth centuries.

From early July until the middle of September, this lovely Georgian spa town is host to a series of festivals, catering for both national and regional audiences and ensuring that Buxton is the liveliest place to be in high summer.

Buxton Well Dressing Festival

Information: ☎ 01298 71352

Starts the summer celebrations. Wells in Buxton are dressed and blessed in inter-denominational services on the second Wednesday in July. The process of dressing the wells can be seen in the Paxton Suite, Pavilion Gardens, on the previous two days. Other events include a fair, a car treasure hunt and a children's concert. Procession through the streets on the following Saturday.

Buxton Festival

Mid-late July. Information: ☎ 01298 70395
Box Office: ☎ 01298 72190

Two-week classical music festival for both opera lovers and critics. Productions of rarely seen works by mainstream composers in the charming Edwardian opera house. Daily programme of events includes concerts, talks, cabaret, lunchtime recitals, public master-classes, Festival masses in St John's Church and the Young Artists series, held in splendid venues throughout the town.

Buxton Festival Fringe

Mid-late July. Information: ☎ 01298 70395

Running alongside the Buxton Festival, the Fringe presents a packed programme of drama, music, comedy, dance, spoken work - in venues all over Buxton; open to all-comers with a full range of entertainment by professional, amateur and student groups; half- and one-day arts workshops during the Festival period.

Buxton Festival of Jazz

Last weekend in July. Information: Peter Johnson, Hon Secretary
☎ 01298 23772

Programme to suit all tastes covering a wide spectrum of Jazz from New Orleans to Modern. Over nine hours of continuous jazz in the Octagon at the Pavilion Gardens, with the audience seated in cabaret style; New Orleans Parade Band procession with an enthusiastic 'second line' following; plus weekend jazz concerts at other venues in the town.

The Opera House is famed for its performances as well as its lovely building adjacent to the Pavilion Gardens

The International Gilbert & Sullivan Festival

First half of August. Information and Box Office: ☎ 01298 72190

International Competition comprising competitive amateur performances under the scrutiny of an expert adjudicator; the Gilbert & Sullivan Opera Company, performing full-scale productions on stage in the Opera House; a festival production — from audition to stage in just one week; fringe events; concerts; recitals; workshops; master-classes; and a children's festival production.

The International Festival of Music Theatre

Beginning of September.
Information and Box Office: ☎ 01298 72190

Opportunity for amateur performers of all ages to participate in a high quality international festival and competition, with master-classes from stars of stage and screen, lectures, workshops, singing and acting competitions. Full-scale, amateur production each evening in the Opera House by a different competing society. Also a Youth Festival of matinees in the Paxton Theatre.

The Spa Town Country Music Festival

Second weekend in September.
Information: Frank Hambleton ☎ 01298 70194

Lively close to Buxton's festival season takes place in the Octagon, Pavilion Gardens, on the Saturday evening and all day Sunday featuring top UK bands.

8 Bakewell & around

Situated at the crossing of the River Wye where the valley widens out, Bakewell is the central town of the Peak and attracts many thousands of visitors. It has interesting groups of buildings and a good selection of shops, both for provisions and souvenirs. Its bookshop carries a wide range of books and papers on the Peak District. Several shops offer Bakewell puddings, preserving the memory of the culinary accident that produced the new dish. The disaster apparently occurred at the Rutland Arms when the cook put the jam at the bottom of the dish instead of (as is usual) on top of the pastry.

Although much of Bakewell has been built since the late nineteenth century, the town centre does have some fine buildings. The **National Park Information Office** is situated in the former Market Hall which dates from the early seventeenth century. Rutland Square — where is now the roundabout — was set out in 1804 when the Rutland Arms was built. This is a fine coaching inn and its stable still remains across the road, the buildings being built around two courtyards, one behind the other.

Behind the Rutland Hotel is a small area of old houses which reward investigation. Just up the road to Monyash (King Street) is the old Town Hall on the right, one of the most interesting buildings in the town. It was built in 1602 and housed the Town Hall upstairs and St John's Hospital on the ground floor.

The Church

Beyond the Town Hall is the church, situated on an elevated site with its steeple dominating the skyline. The west end is Norman, with two surviving arches in what could be the walls of an earlier Saxon building, now the walls between the nave and the adjacent aisles. Much of the present church was built in the thirteenth century but the spire, octagon and south transept (known as The Newark) had to be taken down and rebuilt in the nineteenth century. There are two ancient crosses in the churchyard, of the ninth and eleventh centuries.

Below: Ashford-in-the-Water

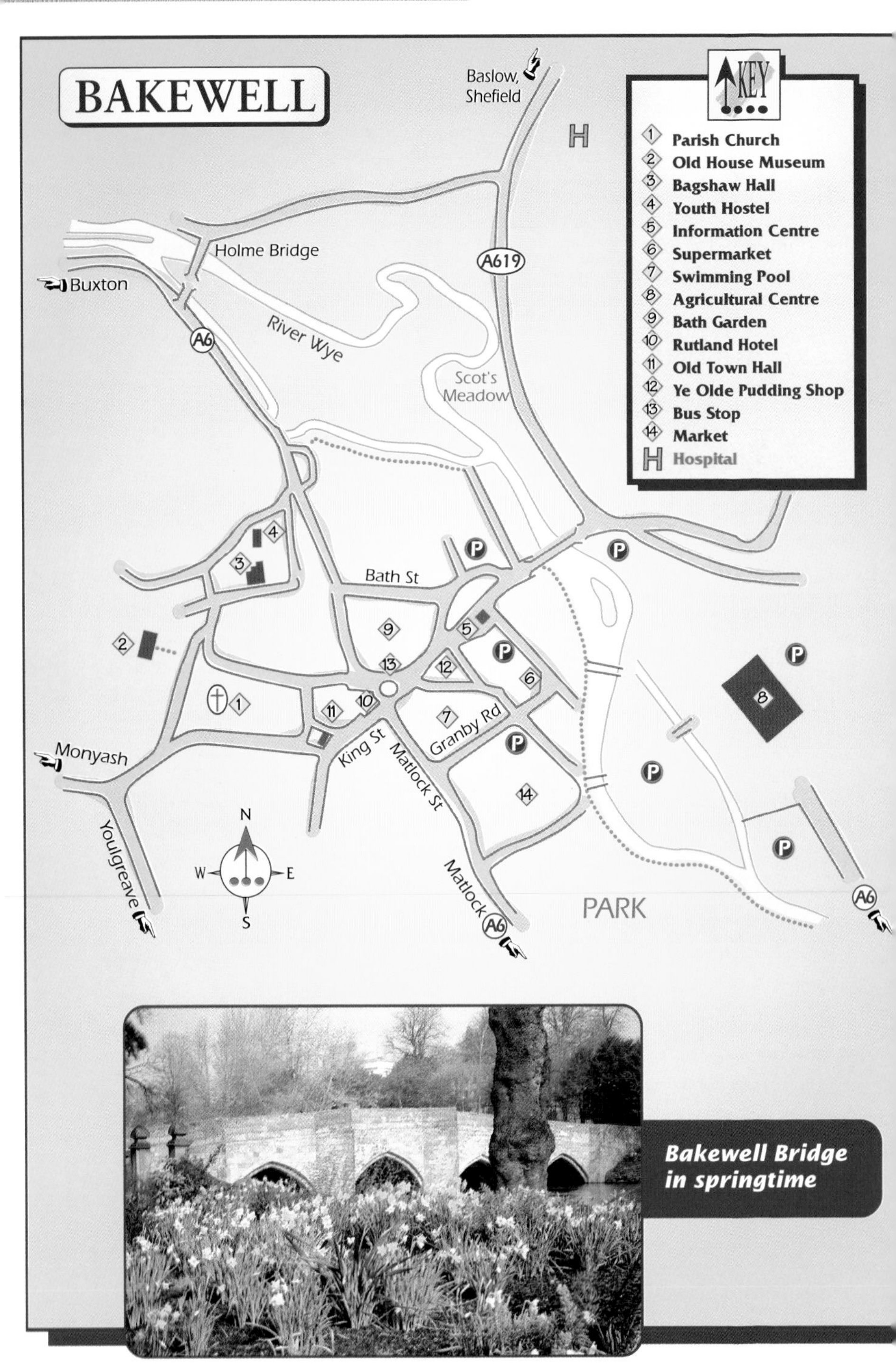

Bakewell Bridge in springtime

Behind and above the church is the **Old House Museum**, constructed in limestone with a stone flagged roof. It was built in 1543 as a parsonage house, extended in about 1620, and was turned into tenements by Sir Richard Arkwright some 250 years later. Bakewell Historical Society started a restoration scheme in 1959. It now displays its original wattle and daub interior walls.

Cunningham Place, Off Church Lane. Folk Museum in historic early sixteenth century house. Historic artifacts and two kitchens, one sixteenth-century and one nineteenth-century. Parties booked for morning or evening visits. ☎ 01629 813165. Open: daily Good Friday to end October, 1.30–4pm. July and August 11am–4pm.

There is a pleasant riverside walk downstream from Castle Street and the bridge. This eventually reaches the park, a large recreation ground with a cricket pitch, football pitch and swings for young children at the far side. If you have your dog with you, this is a pleasant area to exercise it.

Bakewell Show, held annually in August, used to be the largest single day agricultural show in the country but now extends to two days. It is a large event and there are usually many stalls and displays to interest visitors. In addition to craft stalls selling a wide range of quality items there is an enormous marquee with floral displays organised by the Women's Institute. Additionally, of course, there are the stands for farmers and gardeners and the inevitable beer tent! A visit to the show is recommended, but aim to arrive reasonably early — it is very popular!

Haddon Hall

Perhaps the main point of interest of Bakewell is that it acts as a centre for visiting different parts of the Peak and of course the two major houses of the area — Chatsworth and Haddon Hall. The latter lies just down the river from the town and is well worth a visit. It is very much older than Chatsworth, and is claimed by many to be Britain's most complete non-fortified medieval house.

Haddon Hall stands adjacent to the A6, hidden by trees and a beech hedge. The car park is across the road, so that one approaches the gatehouse on foot. The entrance is impressive with two lines of mature beech hedges converging at an old packhorse bridge over the wide but shallow waters of the River Wye. The house itself stands on a bluff overlooking the river and the bridge, although somewhat masked by the trees, and the entrance is at the foot of the north-west tower with a very low doorway.

Haddon Hall

South of Bakewell. Medieval and Tudor manor house with magnificent terraced rose garden. First floor self-service restaurant in the old stable block. Gift shop in the Gate House. Regular Visitors pass available for those visiting several times during the year. Car park 400 yards from the hall. Parking closer than this may be available for the disabled.
☎ 01629 812855.
Open: daily April to September 11am to 6pm. Closed Sundays in August except Bank Holiday Sunday.

The battlemented buildings are set around two courtyards paved with flagstones. In the south-west corner of the Hall and lower courtyard is situated the chapel. This is probably the oldest part of the Hall, for parts of the chapel were built by William Peveril around 1080-90. The altar slab in the south aisle of the chapel is of Norman origin as are the two fonts in other parts of the chapel. It has a three-decker pulpit and various pews built by Sir George Manners in 1624. The chapel is very well lit by natural means and remarkably well preserved

Romantic story

Haddon Hall is, of course, famous for the love story of Dorothy Vernon. Her elopement in 1563 with John Manners was immortalised by Sir Walter Scott, and just off the long gallery one can still see the steps down which she is supposed to have fled, meeting her lover at the little packhorse bridge below the

gardens. Unfortunately, the story is as fictitious as it is romantic, as the long gallery and adjacent garden were built by John and Dorothy 26 years after their marriage; unless, of course, her flight was from a previous building on the site. We shall never know.

The garden at Haddon is always a delight in the summer, especially when the roses and clematis are in bloom. It consists of six large terraces, although unfortunately the upper ones are not open to the public. Judged the 'Garden of the Year' by Christies' and the Historic Houses Association recently, this garden really does justify its reputation.

Rowsley

Continuing down the main valley we come to **Rowsley**. Here the Lathkill joins the Wye at Picory Corner and the combined waters flow towards the Derwent. A small village, Rowsley used to boast a substantial railway marshalling yard — a relic of the days when Rowsley was the rail head of the Midland Railway's line from Derby and prior to the building of the connection with Buxton which began in 1860. It boasts a very fine hotel, the Peacock, originally built in 1652, which later became a dower house of Haddon Hall.

Cauldwell's Mill

At Rowsley, the River Wye joins the Derwent, flowing south from the northern gritstone moors past Calver and Chatsworth. Rowsley also has a working museum at **Caudwell's Mill.** Built in 1875, the mill was originally driven by waterwheels. These were replaced by turbines which still power the machinery. Although some of the original grindstones remain propped against the yard wall, the mill has rolling machinery which replaced the old flour grinding stones.

Caudwell's Mill and Craft Centre

Rowsley, beside A6. Historic water-powered flour mill, café, gift shop, working crafts including wood turner, glass blower, artist, furniture restorer and jewellery gallery. Wholemeal flour always available. Guided tours by arrangement (including evenings) in summer ☎ 01629 734374 (mill) or 733185 (craft centre). Open: daily March to January. Weekends only January and February. April to October 10am–6pm, November to March 10am–4.30pm.

Another group of volunteers has also commenced work in Rowsley; **Peak Rail** has been excavating the site of Rowsley Shed, uncovering the old brick floors and inspection pits. The Society's headquarters are at Darley Dale Station from where short train rides can be enjoyed.

Chatsworth

From Rowsley the River Derwent can be followed upstream to **Chatsworth Park** where there is a convenient free car park at Calton Lees, which can be used to visit the **Chatsworth Garden Centre.** Chatsworth House may be approached from here by walking through the park and alongside the river. Alternatively there is a car park at the opposite end of the park, in Baslow from where a 12 mile (19km) walk leads to the house. Cross the little brook a few yards eastwards from the car park and take the signposted path down the brookside past a rare sight in this area — a thatched cottage. The path crosses the river meadows and reaches Chatsworth by Queen Mary's Bower and the elegant bridge over the river. There is also a car park adjacent to the house itself.

Peak Rail plc

Darley Dale Station, nr Matlock. Enjoy a nostalgic trip up the River Derwent Valley, north of Matlock pulled by steam. Relax in the leisurely atmosphere of the 'Palatine' licensed restaurant car – and enjoy a meal with a difference. Party bookings welcome. ☎ 01629 580381. Open: weekends and Bank Holidays all year round and midweek during the summer months.

Chatsworth House

Historic house and extensive gardens. *Behind the Scenes* days available, advance booking essential. Guided tours by prior arrangement. Shop in former orangery and restaurant and shop in former stable block. Family pass for all attractions available. ☎ 01246 582204. Open: Easter to end of October, 11am–4.30pm, garden 5pm.

Chatsworth, the home of the Cavendish family, is one of the Wonders of the Peak and one of the finest houses in Britain. The son of William Cavendish and Bess of Hardwick was created the first Earl of Devonshire and his descendant, the fourth Earl, was created the first Duke of Devonshire for supporting the cause of William of Orange. Bess of Hardwick brought considerable wealth to the Cavendish family and with the dissolution of the monasteries, this wealth was used to purchase land on a large scale throughout the Peak District and elsewhere.

Today it is open to visitors and the route taken through the house includes the majority of the main state rooms on the south front. Much of the present house was built by the first and sixth dukes, ie in the seventeenth century and in the early part of the nineteenth century. It therefore makes an interesting comparison with the older Haddon Hall. Perhaps one of the most interesting aspects of Chatsworth is that a considerable number of its treasures are on display. Everywhere one goes in the house there are priceless and beautiful works of art. You should allow plenty of time for a walk around Chatsworth. There is so much that otherwise will be missed such as the wood and alabaster carvings in the chapel and the painting of the violin in the music room.

Upon leaving the house a huge conservatory runs up the side of the garden wall, with various fruit trees growing inside. Nearby, although not usually open, is a modern hothouse. It is full of tropical plants including a huge Amazonian lily. Chatsworth is proud that this plant first flowered here in 1851, ahead of the one at Kew!

Queen Mary's Bower

The Garden & Park

The 106 acre (42.4 hectare) garden is also worthy of a visit. It should be given at least half a day in order to explore the various points of interest. These include the Emperor Fountain, which is set in its canal pond and is noted for being the highest gravity fed fountain in the world, rising to a height of 260ft (80m).

Behind the house are the Cascade and the aqueduct, together with Stand Wood with its various footpaths along the valley side. In springtime the woods are full of bluebells and spring flowers. The Cascade has 24 steps and as each one is of varying dimensions, the water makes a different sound as it falls over the steps.

Above the Stand Wood can be seen the Prospect Tower, a relic of the Elizabethan manor house that existed here before the present house was built. A more recent innovation has been the development of a forestry and farming display plus an adventure playground, which is always a special treat for children.

Farmyard and Adventure Playground

Chatsworth. Farming and forestry exhibition and adventure playground. ☎ 01246 582204. Open: daily Easter to end of September, 10.30am–4.30pm, closes 5pm. Adventure playground remains open October, weekends and half-term 12noon–4.30pm.

In May, Chatsworth hosts one of the largest Angling Fairs in Britain, at which there are numerous demonstrations and trade stands. Each September, the Chatsworth Country Fair is held. There is a full programme of events together with over 300 trade stands.

Rambling in the Park

If you like to ramble, do not overlook Chatsworth Park. There are several private paths through the park to which the public are permitted access and these are shown on notice boards. If you are south of the house itself, look out for the deer on the east bank of the river. At Calton Lees picnic area and car park there is a tea bar and the estate sells a leaflet about its Stand Wood walks which take you above and behind Chatsworth House.

In Stand Wood you can walk in comparative quietness around the lakes which supply water to the garden. Quite a long walk can be planned if you so wish. The path climbs up through the wood to the Hunting Lodge.

Edensor

Close to Chatsworth is **Edensor** village, built in 1838-42 by Joseph Paxton to house the inhabitants of the original village. All the houses are of different styles and the church, built in 1867, stands in a dominant situation above the houses. It contains an interesting display on the redevelopment of the village, together with a leaflet for sale explaining much more.

Although it is often thought that the whole of the village — bar one house — was demolished, this is not the case. All the main street was demolished except one house, which now stands in isolation. Several others were altered including the former eighteenth century inn near to the Post Office where there is now a tearoom.

A WALK FROM BAKEWELL

Total distance about 6 miles (9.6km)

A walk with plenty of interest north of Bakewell. Park near Holme Bridge at SK215690 and take the path to the rear of Lumford Cottages. It climbs up through a small plantation adjacent to Holme Bank Chert Mine before cutting across the fields in the direction of Great Longstone. Just north of the little cottage known as Cracknowle House, the path leaves the fields and descends through Cracknowle Wood to Rowdale house and the A6020 from Ashford-in-the-Water to Hassop Station.

Turn left towards Ashford and walk along the road to the junction of the various roads adjacent to the old railway bridge. There is an access road from this junction to Churchdale Farm and on towards Churchdale Hall. The path skirts around the plateau and then drops down a hillside to rejoin the A6020. Walk down the footpath at the side of the road and turn left onto the old and now disused section of the B6465. This has now been re-routed and crosses the River Wye over a new bridge. Upon reaching the A6 a path cuts across the fields on your left and to the north of the A6. There are views towards Ashford Hall and down onto Ashford Lake which runs into the large mill pond of Lumford Mill. This has created quite an elongated and interesting sheet of water in the valley below the path.

Eventually one walks towards a group of houses and the path cuts through the middle of the development to join the A6 once more close to Lumford Mill. There is a short walk down the path at the side of the A6 to Holme Bridge. Here the former sheep wash has been restored and there is an interpretation board which details changes made to the river over the centuries to provide water both for Lumford and Victoria Mills.

Scot's Meadow, Bakewell & the path to Holme Bridge

ACCOMMODATION

Lists of various types of accommodation may be obtained from the following:

Bakewell Tourist Information Office
Old Market Hall, Bridge Street
Bakewell
☎ 01629 813227

Peak & Moorlands Farm Holidays
Lydgate Farm
Aldwark
Grangemill
Wirksworth DE4 4HD
☎ 01629 540250

Derbyshire Dales & Dovedale Farm Holiday Group
Mrs Adams
Park View Farm
Weston Underwood
Derbyshire
☎ 01335 360352

Macclesfield Tourist Information Centre
Town Hall, Market Place
Macclesfield SK10 1HR
☎ 01625 504114

Staffordshire Moorlands Tourist Information Centre
1 Market Place
Leek
Staffs ST13 5HH
☎ 01538 381000

See under 'Tourist Information Centres' for offices where information on accommodation may also be obtained.

Youth Hostels

There are a number of youth hostels in the Peak District. You may join the Youth Hostels Association at the hostel, and it is advisable to book in advance to ensure a bed. Some of England's youth hostels have private rooms, with upgraded facilities. In this area Hartington has rooms with en suite facilities in a separate annexe. Several others have private rooms including Ilam Hall, Gradbach and Matlock.

The YHA runs a Rent-a-Hostel scheme which enables some hostels to be available in the winter season exclusively for private groups. This has proved to be very successful and you may have to book well in advance.

There are youth hostels at Bakewell, Buxton, Dimmingsdale (Oakamoor), Elton, Gradbach, Hartington, Ilam, Matlock, Ravenstor near Miller's Dale, and Youlgreave. Field Study facilities are available at Hartington, Ilam and Gradbach hostels.

Further details are available from:

Youth Hostels Association
Via Gellia Mill
Bonsall
Nr Matlock
Derbyshire
☎ 01629 825850

Camping Barns

The Peak National Park have encouraged the conversion of a number of traditional stone barns into basic low-cost overnight shelter — rather like a stone tent, but with the advantages of weatherproof roof and room to move about! You sleep on a wooden platform; there is a cooking area, table and benches, toilet and a water supply. You are expected to provide all the usual camping equipment, apart from a tent. Those under 18 years old must be accompanied by an adult, and strictly no dogs. There are camping barns at Bakewell, One Ash Grange (Monyash), Birchover, Nab End (Hollinsclough), Warslow, and Butterton (2). Full details, including how to book, are given in a leaflet obtainable from the Peak National Park.

Camping & Caravanning

There are a large number of sites for both tents and caravans. Details can be obtained from the Peak National Park and local tourist information offices.

Cycle Hire

Ashbourne, Mappleton Lane,	☎ 01335 343156
Bakewell, Station Yard,	☎ 01629 814004
Carsington Water, Nr Wirksworth,	☎ 01629 540478 Fax: 01629 540666
Middleton Top, Middleton-by-Wirksworth,	☎ 01629 823204
Parsley Hay, on A515 Ashbourne-Buxton road,	☎ 01298 84493
Waterhouses, Old Station car park,	☎ 01538 308609
Waterhouses, Brown End Farm Leek Road,	☎ 01538 308313

Facilities for the Disabled

For information on the availability of facilities for disabled persons contact the Peak National Park Office ☎ 01629 816200. A booklet entitled *Access for All* is

available from the Peak National Park Office and National Park information centres.

MAPS

The following Ordnance Survey maps cover the areas described in this book:
Landranger 118 *Stoke-on-Trent and Macclesfield 1:50 000*
Landranger 119 *Buxton, Matlock and Dovedale*
Outdoor Leisure 24 *The Peak District ~ White Peak Area*

MARKET DAYS / EARLY CLOSING

Ashbourne: Thursday & Saturday. Some early closing on Wednesday.
Buxton: Tuesday and Saturday. Some early closing on Wednesday.
Bakewell: Monday (and cattle). Some early closing on Thursday.
Matlock: Tuesday and Friday. Some early closing on Thursday.
Wirksworth: Tuesday. Some early closing on Wednesday.

PUBLIC TRANSPORT

There are bus services along most of the major roads across or around the Peak District, but rural services are infrequent or non-existent. Without an annual subsidy of around £96,000 from the Peak National Park Authority, bus and rail services would be much worse than they are.

The main Inter City trains from London stop at Derby, Chesterfield and Sheffield, all of which are convenient for the eastern side of the Peak District. On the western side there are trains from London to Stoke-on-Trent and Manchester via Macclesfield. Trains also run from Manchester to both Buxton and from Derby to Matlock, stopping at stations en route.

If you are planning a visit to the Peak using public transport, you need the 'Derbyshire Peak District Timetable'. It contains details of every bus and rail service in the National Park and is available from Tourist Information Centres in the area or by post from Public Transport Unit, Derbyshire County Council, Chatsworth Hall, FREEPOST, Matlock, DE4 9BR. Additionally the 'Summer Sunday Travel Book' gives details of the summer Sunday and Bank Holiday transport network.

A one-day, unlimited mileage ticket, the *Derbyshire Wayfarer* is available for travel on all local buses and trains throughout Derbyshire.

A useful map of the transport links is on the National Park's 'The Greener Way' leaflet.

RIDING STABLES

Endon Riding School
Coltslow Farm
Stanley Moss Lane
Stockton Brook
Nr Stoke-on-Trent
☎ 01782 502114

Hopkin Farm
Tansley
☎ 01629 582253

Red House Stables
Old Road
Darley Dale
☎ 01629 733583

SAILING

Where sailing is allowed on reservoirs the relevant water authority has delegated responsibility for the sailing on that water to various clubs. In some cases these clubs allow casual visitors and it is necessary to write to the club if you wish to sail there.

Carsington Sailing Club
Carsington Water
Ashbourne
☎ 01629 540609

SHOWS, WELL DRESSING & LOCAL EVENTS

There are many activities going on in the area and the list below includes the majority of those occurring annually.

Local Events and Shows

Ashbourne Shrovetide Football: Shrove Tuesday and Ash Wednesday	
Flagg Races (High Peak Hunt Point to Point): Tuesday after Easter	
Alstonfield Horse Show and Gymkhana	(May)
Chatsworth Angling Fair	(May)
Leek Arts Festival	(May)
Leek May Fair	(May)
Winster Market Fair: Bank Holiday Monday	(May)
Winster Wakes	(June/July)
Ashbourne Carnival	(June/July)
Ashbourne Highland Gathering	(June/July)

Buxton International Arts Festival (June/July)
Leek Club Day (Sunday School and other organisations procession) (June/July)
Leek Show (June/July)
Lyme Park Festival (June/July/August)
Ashbourne Show (August)
Bakewell Show (August)
Crich Tramway Museum, Grand Transport Extravaganza (August)
Cromford Steam Rally (August)
Dovedale Sheepdog Trials (August)
Leek Carnival (August)
Lyme Sheepdog Trials (August)
Macclesfield Forest Chapel Rush Bearing (August)
Manifold Valley Show (August)
Chatsworth Country Fair (September, sometimes end of August)
Hartington Sports (September)
Jenkin Chapel, Saltersford, Harvest Thanksgiving (September)
Lyme Park Horse Trials (September)
Matlock Bath Illuminations and Firework Display (September)

Well Dressing

Middleton-by-Youlgreave (May)
Monyash (May)
Over Haddon (May)
Tissington: Ascension Day until following Monday
Wirksworth (May)

Ashford-in-the-Water	(May/June)
Chelmorton	(June)
Cressbrook	(June)
Mayfield	(June)
Monyash	(June)
Rowsley Well Dressing and Festival	(June)
Tideswell Well Dressing and Wakes Carnival	(June)
Youlgreave	(June)
Bakewell	(June/July)
Bonsall	(June/July)
Bradwell Well Dressing and Gala week	(June/July)
Buxton	(June/July)
Gt Longstone	(June/July)
Little Longstone	(June/July)
Litton	(June/July)
Pilsley	(June/July)
Tideswell	(June/July)
Taddington	(August)
Wardlow	(August)
Wormhill	(August)
Foolow	(August/ September)
Hartington	(September)
Longnor Well Dressing and Sports	(September)
Wormhill	(September)

***Right:* Detail of Well Dressing panel, Tissington**

***Opposite page:* Crich Tramway Museum**

If you would like to see a demonstration of the well dressing art, listed below are the months and contact names. The dates may vary a little from year to year (and also the contact name), but if in doubt, ring the Tourist Information Centre on 01246 345777, or try the nearest Derbyshire Tourist Information Centre to you.

Well Dressing Demonstrations

May:Over Haddon, 10am-5pm at Lathkill Dale Craft Centre
May: Monyash, 7-10pm in Quaker Chapel
(Mrs Edwards ☎ 01629 812778)
May: Middleton-by-Youlgreave, well dressed on site
June: Litton, approximately 10am-10pm
(Mrs Turner ☎ 01298 871569)
July: Buxton, 9am-9pm (until 6pm on 8th) in Paxton Suite, Pavilion Gardens
August: Wormhill, venues signposted
(Mr Peirson ☎ 01298 871023)
August: Wardlow, 1-5pm (Mrs Robinson ☎ 01298 872091)
September: Longnor, 11am-5pm (Mrs Riley ☎ 01298 83495)

SPORTS & OUTDOOR ACTIVITIES

Caving

The many caves and mines should never be entered by the inexperienced. A useful address is:

Peak District Mines Historical Society
c/o Peak District Mining Museum
The Pavilion
Matlock Bath
☎ 01629 583834

Cave Rescue

In an emergncy dial 999 and ask for Cave Rescue.

Walking

Walking is the most popular outdoor activity as the Peak District has walks of all grades of difficulty and length, in fascinating and varied scenery. Some walks are described in this book, or plan your own route with the aid of a large scale OS map. Wear boots or stout shoes (especially on the moors), take weatherproof clothing and a map (and know how to read it correctly).

For those who prefer a guided tour the Peak National Park provides a series of 'Walks with a Ranger' throughout the Peak District. Booking by telephone is essential.
Details from: Peak National Park
☎ 01629 815185 weekends 01433 670216

Squash Courts

There are squash courts at Ashbourne; Leek and Cressbrook Mill, Monsal Dale.

Swimming Pools

There are pools at Leek, Ashbourne, Wirksworth, Buxton, and Matlock.

TOURIST INFORMATION CENTRES

Ashbourne, 13 Market Place,	☎ 01335 343666
Bakewell, Old Market Hall,	☎ 01629 813227
Buxton, The Crescent,	☎ 01298 25106
Leek, 1 Market Place,	☎ 01538 381000
Macclesfield, Town Hall, Market Place,	☎ 01625 504114
Matlock Bath, The Pavilion,	☎ 01629 55082

USEFUL ADDRESSES

Peak National Park Authority
Head Office, Aldern House
Baslow Road
Bakewell
Derbyshire
☎ 01629 816200

The National Park also runs a wide range of residential courses at Losehill Hall. For details write to:

Peak National Park Study Centre
Losehill Hall
Castleton
Derbys S30 2WB
☎ 01433 620373

National Trust
East Midlands Regional Office
Clumber Stableyard
Worksop
Notts S80 3BE

Each year the Peak District National Park publishes a free newspaper. *Peakland Post*, which is available from all information centres and many tourist attractions, hotels etc. It gives up-to-date information on events and visitor attractions within the area.

Index

Published By
Landmark Publishing Ltd
Waterloo House, 12 Compton, Ashbourne,
Derbyshire DE6 1DA England
Tel: 01335 347349 e-mail: landmark@clara.net

1st Edition
ISBN 901 522 27 X

British Library Cataloguing in Publication Data: a catalogue record
for this book is available from the British Library.

Print: UIC Printing & Packaging Pte Ltd, Singapore
Cartography: James Allsopp
Designed by: James Allsopp

Cover Pictures
Front cover: Wetton in spring time
Back cover top: Viator Bridge, Mill Dale, at the northern end of Dove Dale
Back cover bottom: Magpie Mine, Monyash

Picture Credits
James Allsopp: Page 48R, 70 & 90
All other pictures are supplied by the author

Disclaimer
Whilst every care has been taken to ensure that the information in this book is as accurate as possible at the time of publication, the publishers and authors accept no responsibility for any loss, injury or inconvenience subtained by anyone using this book.